NONVIOLENT

ACTION

HANDBOOK

by Sanderson Beck

World Peace Communications

Ojai, California

World Peace Communications was founded
September 1, 2001 as a non-profit corporation
for educational, literary, and charitable purposes.

For more information please contact:

World Peace Communications

World Peace Communications
495 Whitman St. #A
Goleta, CA 93117
worldpeacebooks.org

san@beck.org

Publishers Cataloging-in-Publication Data

Beck, Sanderson, 1947-
    Nonviolent Action Handbook
— 1st ed.
Ojai, California: World Peace Communications, 2003
vi, 96 p. 18 cm.
ISBN 0-9717823-5-0
1. Nonviolence
2. Peaceful change
3. Ahimsa
4. Pacifism
5. Civilian-based defense
I. Title
HM 278 .B42   303.61—dc21   LCCN: 2002117236

CONTENTS

Introduction
1. Nonviolence   1
   Between Submission and Retaliation   1
   Open Friendliness   3
   Honest Communication   4
   Respect for Freedom and Equality   6
   Courageous Compassion   8
   Detached Trusting   10
   Patient Persistence   12
   Politics of Nonviolence   16
   Nonviolence Guidelines   18
   Nonviolence Workshop Agenda   18
   Highlights of Nonviolence in History   20
2. Liberation from Seven Deadly -Isms   25
   Sexism   25
   Racism   27
   Imperialism   29
   Militarism   32
   Materialism   34
   Dogmatism   37
   Egotism   40
3. Group Process   43
   Affinity Groups   43
   Roles in the Affinity Group   45
   Consensus Decision-making   48
   Overcoming Discrimination   54
4. Creative Actions   60
   Investigation and Research   60
   Negotiation or Arbitration   61
   Public Education on the Issue   61
   Vigils and Demonstrations   61
   Boycotts and Strikes   64
   Legal Suits and Noncooperation   64
   Civil Disobedience   65

Fasting   66
Constructive Activity   66
Individual Conscience   68
5. Legal Process   69
Nuremberg Actions or Civil Disobedience   69
Arrest   72
Solidarity   74
Pleading   76
Trial   77
Jail   81
Defense of Necessity   83
International Law Defense   84
War Tax Resistance   93
Building Community   95

Introduction

This Handbook is designed to be a generic guide to nonviolent direct action. In my experience protesting during the 1980s I found that the handbooks published by the Abalone Alliance for protesting the nuclear power plant at Diablo Canyon, California and by the Vandenberg Action Coalition for direct action to stop testing of the MX missile and other handbooks were extremely useful for understanding the methods of nonviolent civil disobedience by affinity groups using consensus decision-making procedures. Much of the information in the chapters on Group Process and Legal Process are drawn from those previous handbooks, and I gratefully acknowledge them. Based on my long studies of peace, nonviolence, politics, international law, social change, and psychological liberation, I have added the chapters on Nonviolence, Liberation from Seven Deadly –Isms, Creative Actions, and also the section on legal defenses using international law. The latter is based on my experience while defending myself in six trials and in writing two appeals to federal circuit courts. This Handbook is generic, because it is not focused on any particular issue or direct action campaign but can be applied to any cause using nonviolent protest. Anyone who has suggestions or questions may communicate with me by sending e-mail to san@beck.org.

The photo on the back cover shows me sitting on the railroad tracks (on the right) blocking a train from the Concord Naval Weapons Station that may have been carrying weapons for shipment to Central America. I have been arrested for protesting nonviolently more than fifty times, and I always felt that the experience was valuable and worth the sacrifice, even when I was imprisoned for six months for having stepped over an imaginary line outside the main gate of the Trident submarine base at King's Bay, Georgia in 1989. How long it will take to bring peace and justice to this world will probably depend on how many people are willing to make such sacrifices and to work also in other ways to reform our violent society. Mahatma Gandhi called his nonviolent efforts to improve society his experiments with truth, and I encourage you to make such experiments also by courageously putting your love into practice.

I believe that our violent and plutocratic society needs a nonviolent revolution to end the neo-imperialist policies of the United States Government by democratic means so that we can have governments of real compassion, liberty, and true justice for all. This transformation of militarism must be nonviolent, not only because any violent attempt would be crushed by force, but because we are opposed to using violence. This ultimate revolution of our historic era is essentially a revolution to end the use of massive force in wars as instruments of social and political control. The process is one of converting hearts and minds by demonstrating the better ways of using education, communication, democracy, and active nonviolent persuasion. As George Harrison sang, "With our love we can change the world, if they only knew." I have faith that the actions of loving people will bring about a more peaceful society. I hope you will help.

* *

The only solution is love.
Dorothy Day

* *

1

Nonviolence

The way of love, or nonviolence, as Mahatma Gandhi once said, is as old as the hills. The English word "nonviolence" derives conceptually from the Sanskrit word *ahimsa*, which literally means not hurting. The root of this word is *hins*, a desiderative form of *han*, which means to slay, kill, or damage. Thus *hins* implies the desire to kill, injure or destroy. The *a* is a negative giving *ahimsa* the broader meaning of not having any desire, wish, or will to kill, injure or destroy.

If people are hurting, injuring, or killing others, those of us who feel a concern to alleviate or eliminate that suffering being inflicted have the right, if we choose to exercise it, to attempt to intervene to prevent or stop the harm. Yet our first concern and responsibility is to make sure that we are not adding to the harm being done— thus the importance of strictly adhering to the principle of nonviolence in whatever we do. Our love and compassion for those suffering or about to suffer may move us to act in a nonviolent manner to help. Everyone is not obligated to do this, and we cannot force anyone to support us in this effort.

Between Submission and Retaliation

The way of nonviolent action has been described as a third way, an alternative to weak submission to wrongs and violent reaction against them. Most people only see the two common alternatives: they either accept the unjust situation passively or prepare to use force in defense of their rights. Unfortunately those who use force often are not able to control it or keep it from oppressing others. Thus what starts out as a means of defending a group's interests often ends up interfering in the affairs of others. Justice is rarely achieved by seeing who has the strongest military forces to kill and destroy the opponent most effectively. On the other hand those who passively submit to what is forced upon them usually are considered weak and cowardly as they suffer oppression from the aggressive.

The third way enables even those who are few in numbers or poor in material resources to stand up for their rights with moral strength and dignity. Also neutral persons may come to their aid without injuring either side, and even dissenters from the aggressive side may intervene nonviolently for the sake of justice. One need not be big and powerful by worldly standards to use nonviolent action. The very old and young, women, and even the handicapped can be just as effective in non-violent action as physically strong young men. The power of nonviolence comes from the spiritual qualities of love, understanding, communication skill, courage, and persistent endurance.

Regardless of the particular goal or cause at stake, the nonviolent method is careful to make sure the means do no harm. By not inflicting any harm on the opponents the nonviolent activists are not immediately threatening to them. However, the opponents may not like the goals of the nonviolent action, and therefore they may inflict harm on the nonviolent people anyway. When this occurs, it is important that peaceful activists not retaliate or fight back physically. At the same time it is equally important that we persist in our efforts and not give in because of the suffering we are undergoing. Otherwise we are encouraging the opponents to punish us in order to "deter" us. In this way nonviolent activists can earn the respect of opponents who believe in force. As they realize that force is not working in stopping the activists' protests, they will have to re-evaluate their tactics and the whole situation. Using nonviolent action is no guarantee that no violence will result, because the opponents may use force. However, it is the strongest form of action that we can use to truly win over the opponents, while minimizing the total violence by not contributing to it at all. The weak method of passive submission does nothing to alleviate the oppression and injustice already present, while violent reaction escalates the violence and oppression of the situation.

Open Friendliness

The way of nonviolence is open to the flow of love which may come from any direction. To love completely is to be open to the whole universe and everyone in it, both in receiving from others and in giving love to others. True love is universal, not just for one other person. By being open and friendly to everyone we can better understand them and their concerns, and they will be more likely to listen to ours as well. The way of love treats the whole world as one big happy family. In this way we do not close ourselves off from anyone or any viewpoint. We are not afraid to consider all views, and we find that diversity does not have to result in disharmony if we are friends.

In the nonviolent movement we are very friendly toward each other; at the same time we try to be equally friendly toward our opponents and critics. As human beings they are just as important as we are, and we need to understand them even more than people who agree with us. What the world needs more than anything else is more love and friendship, and this is something that each of us can contribute to in our daily lives. By developing friendly relationships with those who oppose us we are beginning the process of social healing. Nothing is more disarming than a sincere smile.

Openness means that we are not trying to hide anything or take advantage of what the other person does not know. Also it means that we are open to receive what other people have to offer us. We are open to the flow of Spirit moving in our lives and in the lives of those around us. We are available to communication and relationship and cooperation with what is good. However, in our openness to examine all viewpoints, we still retain our own discernment of what is morally good. We need not agree with all concepts or attitudes nor do we cooperate with what we believe is harmful, but we are always willing to discuss and consider what is best.

Friendliness is a good feeling that we share with others. When our hearts are open, we do not discriminate between people but share our good feelings with everyone equally. In this way we live in love all the time. Yet we do not need to love what everyone does. We can discern the difference between our love for people and what they do. We may hate their actions and attitudes but still love them as souls and human beings. In fact loving friendship is not afraid to communicate our concerns and differences of opinions so that we might resolve them most easily and directly. Sometimes this requires "hard love" and honesty in communication.

Honest Communication

Gandhi used the term *satyagraha* to describe the way of the nonviolent activist. The word *satya* means truth, deriving from *sat* which means truth in the sense of being, reality or existence. The word *graha* means firmly holding to something. Thus *satyagraha* means firmly holding to the truth and implies that this truth is the spiritual reality of our beingness, as when Jesus said, "I am life, truth, and the way." Regardless of a person's religion or lack of it, this nonviolent way is based on a spiritual dedication to truth and therefore honesty in human relations.

The great gift of our human intelligence enables us to communicate clearly with each other, not only directly by our actions but also symbolically by means of language. Because language is a symbolic abstraction referring to objects, relations, and concepts, the words may or may not be accurate to the reality they are attempting to describe. In other words, language may be in error, or people can and do lie. Deception is a subtle form of violence, because it shows a lack of respect for other people or fear of reality. The way of love is based on the love of the truth in everyone and everything. Gandhi used to say that there is no God higher than the truth. To separate ourselves from the truth is to separate ourselves from reality.

Thus to be true to ourselves we must be true to others as well. Is it really loving to try to be nice and not to tell someone we like that what they are doing is bothering us? If we allow resentment to build up, we soon find ourselves in conflict and misunderstanding. True love means having the courage to confront ourselves and others with the reality of what is going on so that we can work to resolve it together. By hard love we learn how to be self-critical and constantly watchful of how we can improve ourselves and our situation with others.

Our feelings tell us much about what is going on with us, and by communicating them we will be much more able to master the situation in a way that is best for the group. Of course this does not mean we unleash all our personal problems on others without any discernment. The best communication is clear, open, and honest. We clearly communicate when we are aware of what our feelings, thoughts, and concerns are and make them clear to others without inflicting our own "stuff" on to other people. We are responsible for working out our own emotional problems without projecting them on others, but we can still communicate what we are going through if we wish. We need to be careful not to let personal problems distort the larger issues we are working on together. The process of group communication can help us each to see past our own personal concerns to what is best for everyone.

As a group it is especially important that we make sure that our communications with the public and our adversaries are accurate and truthful, because the credibility of our movement depends on this trust that we are not trying to mislead people. This is another contrast to the military methods of secrecy and surprise. In making peace with others we want them to know exactly what we are doing and what our objectives are so that we can work them out in as open a situation as possible. How much information a group decides to volunteer to opponents is an issue to be discussed in relation to strategy. However, there can be little doubt that conscious deception must be prohibited for the sake of public trust.

Respect for Freedom and Equality

The way of love is also the way of freedom, because no one but ourselves directs us how to express our love. This is another contrast to military authoritarianism in which individuals must take orders from superiors. In the nonviolent movement we are all free and equal, each listening to our own inner guidance and sharing our concerns with the group. Then the group can freely decide, based on all individuals' considerations, how the group wishes to act. Thus first we must recognize our own freedom of choice and equal right to participate.

Even more important is that we realize the equality of all human beings and respect the liberty of others just as we want our own freedom respected. The nonviolent way of love is not possessive of others nor does it attempt to control others or use force against them. If we love others, we respect their autonomy to make their own decisions. We certainly can communicate with them, and we may even confront them with our presence to pressure them nonviolently to make a specific choice, if we believe that what they are doing is wrong and harmful to people. The important distinction is that we do not try to force them physically or violently to do what we want. Rather we may attempt to intervene non-violently between the persons and the wrong acts we believe they are doing so that they have to make a choice either to remove us or stop that behavior. Non-violent protests do not hurt people, although they may cause them some inconvenience in going about the busi-ness which we believe is harmful. In doing this we attempt to treat these people as our equals and respect them as individuals. Our actions are meant as a direct communication of our concern for the well-being of those involved in the situation.

We must be careful in our attitudes not to imply that we feel we are superior, because we are critical of what others are doing. We all make mistakes, and the non-violent way is a path of humility which attempts to peacefully suggest to others that they may wish to examine the morality of what they are doing. We are not insisting that they change, but we may insist that they at least consider changing. We do this by presenting them with clear choices, which often result in our own self-sacrifice if they make the choice we believe is wrong. Thus we have not inflicted suffering on them, but we have been willing to suffer in our attempt to alleviate the wrong.

Courageous Compassion

Contrary to much popular belief, the way of love and nonviolent action is not a weak and passive method, and it certainly is not for cowards. Nonviolent direct action may take more courage than fighting with violence in a war, although that is a kind of bravery. However, if we analyze the use of weapons we can see that they are employed out of fear of what the opponent will do to us if we do not use violence against them. The truly courageous are not afraid of the opponents and therefore need no weapon at all. Does it take more courage to go into battle hiding behind armor and using a gun to kill anyone who appears threatening or to walk with dignity unarmed and unafraid into the conflict?

Thus courage is measured by how much we are able to overcome our fear and do what we believe is best to do anyway. Those who fight with weapons for what they believe are more courageous than those who passively accept injustice and allow themselves to be controlled by those who are threatening them. Yet the most courageous are those who stand up to injustice and actively work to change it by nonviolently intervening using purely moral courage and no physical weapons for defense. The most courageous do not kill out of fear of others but are willing to die if necessary for what is right. Love and trust, not hate and fear, are the real marks of the truly courageous. The word "courage" comes from the French word for heart *(coeur)*. Do we have the heart to expose ourselves to our opponents trusting in a human and nonviolent process of reconciliation?

Compassion is what gives us this heart. Compassion

may be defined as the love which not only empathizes with others in feeling what they are going through, but also is wise and courageous enough to do something about it. Thus compassion is love in action and is willing to take on the suffering of others in order to redeem them and those who are doing wrong to them. In compassion we have progressed beyond anger and hate of those who are doing wrong through pity and into mercy and caring and healing. Compassion comes from an experience of oneness with others which expands our hearts so that we feel what people are suffering and are moved to help them.

When we discover that people are dying of starvation or suffering chronic malnutrition at the same time as the world has surplus food and is wasting its resources, then compassion tells us we must work to alleviate this situation. When we see our government using vast financial, technical, and human resources oppressing poor people in other countries and threatening all nations on the earth with genocidal weapons, then compassion tells us that it is our responsibility to change our nation's priorities from death and exploitation to life and sharing. When we see the natural environment deteriorating and this generation robbing the resources from the future, then compassion tells us that we must learn to live more in harmony with the Earth and plan for our children's health and well-being. When we hear of individuals caught in a web of propaganda and exploitation, not realizing the harm they are doing nor seeing any other way out from their predicament, then compassion tells us we must communicate to them the alternatives which are better for all of us. When we know in our hearts that we can make a contribution for the betterment of humanity, then compassion tells us that we must move into action.

Detached Trusting

The way of love is based on the faith that if we act in a good way without harming anyone, then inevitably in the long run the results will be good. Instead of trying to control people by threats and force of might we allow humans to use intelligence to solve our problems by communication and negotiation. We may trust in God, or the process of the universe, as well as in human abilities. By challenging our opponents unarmed we are demonstrating our trust in them that they will not destroy us. By standing up to the wrongs we believe they are doing, we are trusting that by a nonviolent process those wrongs will eventually be redressed. Ultimately even if our bodies are destroyed, we will have done what was right and would be trusting that in the future people would recognize that and right the wrongs eventually.

In order to trust fully we must let go of our own control of the situation and allow others to participate in the process. If we are attached to achieving certain results, then we may prejudge the process and reject the will of the Spirit of the whole. The situation may not be best resolved in exactly the way we think it should. Of course we can have goals and objectives for our action; but once we have defined the purpose of our action we need to be detached from the specific results along the way. Otherwise we will find ourselves disappointed and discouraged. The *Bhagavad-Gita* teaches non-attachment to the fruits of action. That means that it is important that we act for the good without worrying about whether we are immediately successful, and also that we should not be concerned about receiving any credit or reward for our work. Jesus spoke about the same thing when he taught how the selfless person desires no personal reward; the rewards come spiritually (inwardly) or "in heaven."

Of course being detached and trusting does not mean we should trust blindly. We must monitor what is going on and be working toward our objectives constantly. To trust people is not necessarily to let them take advantage of us. We must watch what they do. If they betray their word or deceive us, then we can point that out to them and others. We can continue to protest the wrongs they are doing while informing the general public. Our own integrity is always within our own control. We can love others unconditionally, but we do not have to reward people for doing wrongs. In that case we do not withdraw our love for them, but we can withdraw our cooperation from the wrongs we believe they are perpetrating.

Detachment enables us to be free within ourselves from emotional clinging to people or specific experiences. It does not mean that we do not care, because we can show that we care by our actions. To be detached means that we are not controlled by others or by conditioning or by the situation. We are free enough to transcend our fears, desires, aversions, ambitions, etc. and perceive what is truly best for all concerned. This equanimity or even-mindedness gives us peace within ourselves that we can then share with others by being calm and in control of ourselves in any situation.

However, this does not preclude the feeling or expressing of emotion through compassion or other passions; but instead of being controlled by the emotions we are aware of them and in control of them so that we can use our feelings in our communication with others. So when the situation calls for it we may weep in sorrow or joy, or shout assertively to protest a terrible situation. These feelings will not destroy our detachment if they are authentic feelings, we are aware of what is going on, and we are controlling their expression by channeling the emotional energy in such a way that it is not harming anyone but is communicating a proper concern. Feelings are very powerful means of communication, and often we need to pay more attention to them, not less. To suppress consciously or repress unconsciously our inner feelings is not detachment nor is it healthy. If more people would listen and act on our truer and deeper feelings, our society might not be as sick as it is today. Thus we can distinguish the difference between the prevalent psychic numbing in the face of our overwhelming problems and the detachment which enables us to act freely and intelligently.

Patient Persistence

Nonviolent activist Jim Douglass referred to patience as a revolutionary virtue. Others may criticize us as impatient, because we feel the need to take direct action rather than let a slower evolutionary process occur. Patience is not an excuse for not acting, but rather a quality that helps us to endure and persist in our efforts while proceeding in a calm and intelligent manner. When we are caught up in action, the emotions are often very active and sometimes turbulent. We must be careful not to react without thinking very carefully about what we are doing and what the consequences are likely to be. Patience gives us time for deliberation and reflection on the issues and how our actions can be both nonviolent and yet effective. It is better to wait and perhaps miss a small opportunity of the moment than to rush into something foolishly or unprepared. New opportunities always come forward. If we think out the situation and how we can best deal with it, the next time it occurs we will be ready to act in a good way.

Unlike military action which strikes quickly and ruthlessly, nonviolent action is slow and deliberate with ample warning given to the opponents so that they can consciously decide how they wish to meet our confrontation. We do not want our opponents to have to react quickly with instinctive reflexes. We want them to know us and our methods so that they can respond as calmly and as intelligently as possible.

Military methods are quick and destructive like fire, but nonviolent action is flowing and nurturing like water that nourishes growing things. For some crazy reason people say, "Fight fire with fire," but does it not make much more sense to fight fire with water? The flow of water follows the lowest path, but by flowing constantly for a long time it wears away the hardest rocks. To be successful, nonviolent movements must continuously persist until the opposition's hard hearts have melted, and we have achieved a higher level of cooperation. After Gandhi returned to India from South Africa, where he spent twenty years developing his nonviolent methods, it took thirty years before India won her independence from Great Britain. Women in the United States worked for the right to vote from 1848 until they achieved it in 1920. The way for a nonviolent movement to lose is to stop the effort. As long as we persist, we will make progress in communication, education, and awakening of the public to the circumstances we want changed. The quicker way to lose is to become violent and lose moral credibility. When we act nonviolently, the opponents may arrest us or allow us to stop the wrong we are acting to stop; either way we win attention to our cause and make it more difficult for them to continue those wrongs.

Persistence also means that we must be flexible in our strategy and tactics. If one method does not work, we should let it go and try another. If one issue has been resolved successfully, then we can go on to the next in importance. If one avenue seems to be blocked, we can flow to another area that needs attention. If people seem to be losing interest, we can be creative with new and interesting approaches to the problems. If we feel we are burned out, we can take a break to replenish our spiritual and inner resources and come back with renewed energy. We need to persist not only in our efforts for social change; but even more important we must persist in our love for one another, for this above all will sustain us.

The way of love is always patient and forgiving but at the same time persistent in doing good. When people admit they have done wrong, we can achieve reconciliation by forgiving them. The ultimate goal of nonviolent action is not victory over the opponents but the finding of a harmonious way of living together peacefully with justice. We seek no advantage over anyone else. We are working for the good of our adversaries just as much as for ourselves. Thus when we are successful, everyone will be the victors; and those who have become converted to a better way of life will truly deserve just as much credit, if not more, for their transformation as those who worked to stimulate that change. The way of love leads to a society in which freedom and equality and justice and friendly relationships between all people become the norm, what might be called the reign of God, spiritual democracy, or paradise on Earth. Since we would be very fortunate indeed to achieve these goals within our lifetime, we will need a great amount of patience and persistence.

* *

For we no longer take up 'sword against nation'
nor do we 'learn war any more,' having become children of peace,
for the sake of Jesus, who is our leader.
Origen

* *

The alternative to violence is nonviolent resistance....

First, this is not a method for cowards; it does resist.
The nonviolent resister is just as strongly opposed to the evil
against which one protests as is the person who uses violence....
This method is passive physically but strongly active spiritually....

A second point is that nonviolent resistance
does not seek to defeat or humiliate the opponent,
but to win their friendship and understanding....

A third characteristic of this method is
that the attack is directed against forces of evil
rather than against persons who are caught in those forces.
It is evil we are seeking to defeat,
not the persons victimized by evil....

A fourth point that must be brought out
concerning nonviolent resistance is that
it avoids not only external physical violence
but also internal violence of spirit.
At the center of nonviolence stands the principle of love.
In struggling for human dignity
the oppressed people of the world must not allow themselves
to become bitter or indulge in hate campaigns.
To retaliate with hate and bitterness
would do nothing but intensify the hate in the world.
Along the way of life, someone must have sense enough
and morality enough to cut off the chains of hate.
This can be done only by projecting the ethics of love
to the center of our lives....

Finally, the method of nonviolence is based on the conviction
that the universe is on the side of justice.
It is this deep faith in the future
that causes the nonviolent resister
to accept suffering without retaliation....

World peace through nonviolent means
is neither absurd nor unattainable.
All other methods have failed,
Thus we must begin anew....

We have the choice in this world today
between nonviolence and non-existence.
Martin Luther King, Jr.
* *

Experiment with nonviolent struggle has barely begun.
But in a world in which traditional violent battle
can escalate into nuclear war,
it is an experiment that is absolutely necessary
to push to its furthest limits.
Barbara Deming
* *

Politics of Nonviolence

(Note: This section is from an earlier Nonviolence hand-book and has been adapted from *The Politics of Nonviolent Action* by Gene Sharp.)

The conventional view of political power sees people as dependent on the good will and caprice of their government and any other hierarchical system to which they belong. Power is seen as something people have; kings, czars, generals hold power as one holds a knife. Power resides in knowledge, control of wealth and in the ability to impose violence. Those who serve have little power. Consequently, those without power must kill or destroy their rulers and replace them in their positions in order to wield the selfsame power.

The theory of active nonviolence proposes a different analysis: that government depends on people and that political power is variable, even fragile, always dependent on the cooperation of a multitude of groups and individuals. The withdrawal of that cooperation restricts and can even dissolve power. Put another way, power depends on continuing obedience; thus when we refuse to obey our rulers, their power begins to crumble.

In this sense, nonviolent action is not passive, nor is it a naive belief in converting the opposition, nor is it a "safe" method of protest, immune from repression. Rather, it is based on a different understanding of where people's power really lies. By disobeying, people learn to withhold, rather than surrender, their cooperation. This recognizes that the individual's discovery of self-respect is tied to the recognition that one's own assistance makes the unjust regime possible. When a large enough group of people recognizes this, as the "untouchables" did with Gandhi's help, the result is massive noncooperation and obstruction involving the use of social, economic, and political power.

Then why don't people decide to withdraw cooperation? Why instead do so many obey so few? and how can this change? The authorities are able to wield power both because masses of people passively obey, and because they have the violent means for suppressing dissent— police, National Guard, prison guards and prison cells. A few disobey and are punished, keeping many afraid.

Yet there are chinks in the armor. First, the repressive apparatus is made up of human beings, whose cooperation is essential. A nonviolent approach to the police undercuts their rationale for violence and reveals to neutral parties the extent to which the system relies on violence and force. Second, the repressive apparatus can only survive with a minimal level of dissent (either much mild dissent or a small number of militant dissenters). When dissent grows and brings pressure to bear, the system breaks down. When a nonviolent campaign stands its ground using nonviolence to resist dispersal (not merely for a day or a weekend but over time), it greatly raises the cost of continuing violence against it until it is no longer feasible.

Nonviolence Guidelines

1. We will not harm anyone, and we will not retaliate in reaction to violence.

2. We will be honest and will treat every person with respect, especially law officers.

3. We will express our feelings but will not harbor hatred.

4. We will be alert to people around us and will provide needed assistance.

5. As peacekeepers we will protect others from insults and violence.

6. During a demonstration we will not run nor make threatening motions.

7. If we see a demonstrator threatening anyone, we will intervene to calm down the situation. If demonstrators become violent, and we cannot stop it, we will withdraw.

8. We will not steal, and we will not damage property.

9. We will not carry any weapons.

10. We will not bring or use any alcohol or drugs, other than for medical purposes.

11. We will keep the agreements we make with other demonstrators. In the event of a serious disagreement, we may withdraw.

12. We will accept responsibility for our nonviolent actions, and we will not lie nor use deception to escape the consequences of our actions.

Nonviolence Workshop Agenda

5 min. **Introduction of Facilitators**.

5 min. **Agenda Review**.

30 min. **Slideshow or Video Presentation**.

20 min. **Introductions and Sharing**. People give their names and organizations and share briefly their concerns about the issue.

30 min. **Philosophy and History of Nonviolence**. This may include a brainstorm on what nonviolence is or how it has been used effectively, as well as some lecture and discussion.

5 min. **Nonviolence Guidelines or Discipline**.

10 min. **Break**.

10 min. **Present Active Listening Skill**.

20 min. **Discuss Nonviolence in Triads**. In groups of three, people share their personal feelings about nonviolent action by responding to questions, such as "What are the qualities of nonviolence you personally hope to embody?" and "What is leading you to nonviolently protest?" Each person speaks in turn as the other two actively listen.

20 min. **Hassle Line Role-play**. The group divides in half and forms two parallel lines facing each other. One line plays the role of opponents or the police, while the other line is demonstrators attempting to communicate their concerns. Switch roles.

10 min. **Scenario**. Review plans for anticipated direct action.

30 min. **Meal Break**.

30 min. **Consensus Process and Affinity Groups**. Discuss how consensus works and what affinity groups are.

15 min. **Consensus Role-play**. Group struggles through the process of coming to consensus on some decision, such as agreeing to the Nonviolence Discipline.

15 min. **Affinity Group Quick Decision-making Role-play**. Group is faced with a situation, such as police brutality in an action and must decide quickly as a group how to respond.

30 min. **Legal Briefing**. Discuss legal options and possible consequences.

10 min. **Break**.

20 min. **Direct Action Role-play**. Assign and play out

the roles involved in an arrest situation to include people risking arrest, supporters, military personnel, law enforcement officers, media reporters, counter-demonstrators, etc. Share feelings afterwards.

20 min. **Jail Conditions**. Discuss local jail conditions and share feelings concerning incarceration.

20 min. **Solidarity Issues**. Discuss options of cite release, bail, fines, probation, etc. in regard to strategies of refusing certain options for group empowerment.

10 min. **Affinity Group Formation**. Find out if individuals are in Affinity Groups or whether they would like to form one or more out of the Preparation.

10 min. **Evaluation and Closing Circle**. Share feelings.

Highlights of Nonviolence in History

(Note: This section is taken mostly from *Guides to Peace and Justice* by Sanderson Beck and indicates some of the highlights in that book.)

c. 2050 BC King Bilalama formulated the Eshnunna law code.

1848-1806 BC Hammurabi ruled Babylon with a law code.

c. 1275 BC Moses led Hebrew slaves out of Egypt.

742-697 BC Isaiah and Micah prophesied in Israel and Judah.

c. 700 BC Parshva taught nonviolence in India.

682 BC Athenian kingship was reduced to annual election.

c. 600-551 BC Zarathushtra taught a new religion in Persia.

627-580 BC Jeremiah prophesied in Judah.

594 BC Solon was elected archon and revised laws for Athens.

545 BC Heang Seu organized a peace conference at Song.

531-510 BC Pythagoras taught at Crotona.

528-483 BC Buddha taught in India.

521-479 BC Confucius taught humanistic ethics.

c. 520 BC Lao-zi wrote *Dao De Jing* in China.

519-490 BC Mahavira taught nonviolence in India.

509 BC Rome became a republic.

494 BC Roman plebeians asserted rights and elected tribunes.

462 BC Pericles led democratic reforms in Athens.

432-393 BC Mo-zi and his disciples intervened to stop wars.

425-405 Euripides' tragedies protested the Peloponnesian War.

424-405 BC Aristophanes' comedies protested the same war.

403 BC Socrates refused to obey the 30 tyrants ruling Athens.

399 BC Socrates was the first philosopher to be publicly executed.

355 BC Isocrates criticized Athenian imperialism in *On the Peace*.

320-310 BC Confucian Mencius advised Qi king Xuan.

261-236 BC Ashoka applied Buddhist principles in ruling India.

70 BC Cicero prosecuted Verres for corruption in Sicily.

44-43 BC Cicero's "Philippics" criticized Antony.

c. 27-30 CE Jesus taught and healed in Israel.

c. 30 CE Jesus was crucified by Romans at Jerusalem.

202 Christians were martyred for religious belief in Carthage.

249-251 Christians did not fight back when persecuted by Decius.

303 Christians did not fight back when persecuted by Diocletian.

989 Church council at Charroux declared the Peace of God.

1047 Truce of God was proclaimed at Caen for Normandy.

1073-1085 Hildebrand as Pope Gregory VII opposed Heinrich IV.

1167-1279 Cathars were persecuted by the Albigensian Crusade.

1215 King John was persuaded to sign the *Magna Carta*.

1219 Francis of Assisi on a crusade preached against war.

1231-1273 Sufi Rumi taught mystical love and whirling dance.

1259 Louis IX abolished judicial duels in France.

1392-1398 Chinese planted one billion trees.

c. 1400 The Hopi lived peacefully north of Mexico.

c. 1420-1460 Peter Chelcicky taught nonviolence.

1489-1536 Erasmus wrote extensively against war.

1501-1539 Nanak founded the Sikh religion.

1525 Anabaptists formed a nonviolent church.

1526 Nonviolent Hutterite communities began.

1544 Peaceful Mennonites began following Menno Simons.

1572 Dutch Mennonites refused to go to war.

1651 "Quaker" George Fox was jailed during the civil war.

1682-1756 Pennsylvania had a pacifist government.

1760-1775 Nonviolent phase of the American revolution.

1765 American colonists disobeyed the Stamp Act.

1773 Merchants dressed as Indians dumped tea in Boston harbor.

1815 Peace societies were founded in England and America.

1838 Garrison founded the New England Non-Resistance Society.

1838 Emerson lectured on war to the American Peace Society.

1843 Peace Congresses began being held in Europe.

1845 Elihu Burritt began advocating passive resistance.

1846 Thoreau was arrested for not paying a war tax.

1846 Adin Ballou published *Christian Non-Resistance*.

1848 Woman's Rights Conference was held at Seneca Falls.

1849 Thoreau published "Resistance to Civil Government."

1850-1867 Deak led Hungarian struggle against Austrian empire.

1858 Lucy Stone refused to pay taxes.

1869 Imprisoned Bahá'u'lláh sent prophetic tablets.

1872 Susan B. Anthony was arrested for voting in Rochester.

1890 Sioux ghost dancers were massacred at Wounded Knee.

1893-1910 Tolstoy wrote about love and nonviolence.

1894-1914 Gandhi helped Indians win rights in South Africa.

1905, 1917 Nonviolent phases of the Russian revolution.

1906 Gandhi used first massive civil disobedience.

1906-1918 Pankhursts led suffragette campaign in England.

1909 Jailed suffragettes went on hunger strikes.

1911-1913 'Abdu'l-Bahá spoke in Europe and America.

1914 Fellowship of Reconciliation was founded.

1915-1935 Jane Addams led WILPF.

1917 American Friends Service Committee was founded.

1917-1919 Alice Paul led the Woman's Party direct action.

1918 Bertrand Russell was imprisoned for pacifist writing.

1919 Gandhi called a general strike in India.

1920 Berlin nonviolently defeated a rightist coup.

1921 Gandhi led noncooperation to end untouchability.

1923 War Resisters League was founded.

1928 Einstein advised refusing military service.

1930 Gandhi led salt march and civil disobedience.

1933 Dorothy Day founded the Catholic Worker.

1936-1937 CIO strikes used sit-down tactic at General Motors.

1940-1945 Denmark and Norway resisted Nazi occupation.

1940-1953 A. J. Muste led the Fellowship of Reconciliation.

1947 India and Pakistan gained independence nonviolently.

1947 Pax Christi International was founded.

1948-now Costa Rica has no military forces.

1953 300,000 East German workers went on strike.

1955-1956 Montgomery bus boycott desegregated buses.

1955-1965 Nonviolent protests won civil rights legislation.

1955-1961 Catholic Workers refused to obey civil defense drills.

1956 Hungarians changed their leader but were crushed.

1957 SANE was founded to protest nuclear weapons.

1958 Schweitzer made radio broadcasts on atomic weapons.

1959 King organized Southern Christian Leadership Conference.

1960 Russell led 5,000 in sit-down protest of Polaris.

1961 Women Strike for Peace began protesting.

1963 King wrote a letter from the Birmingham jail.

1963-1973 Protesting eventually stopped U.S. war in Vietnam.

1964 Mario Savio led Free Speech Movement at Berkeley.

1964-1965 Civil Rights Act and Voting Rights Act passed.

1968 Czechoslovakia experimented with nonviolent reforms.

1968 Catonsville 9 led by Berrigans burned draft records.

1968 Protesters disrupted Democratic Convention in Chicago.

1969 Greenpeace began using nonviolent direct action.

1969 Large demonstrations deterred Vietnam War escalation.

1976 Thousands protested nuclear power in Wyhl, West Germany.

1977 1,414 were arrested at Seabrook, New Hampshire.

1977 Argentina mothers of disappeared protested.

1979 200 blocked the first Trident submarine at Groton.

1979 250 blockaded at Rocky Flats, Colorado.

1980 Poland's Solidarity Union began and grew to ten million.

1980-now Plowshares actions disarmed nuclear weapons.

1980 Thousands of dolphins blocked Japanese fishing boats.

1980-1990 Sanctuary movement took in "illegal" Salvadorans.

1981 1,900 were arrested at Diablo Canyon, California.

1981-2000 Women protested missiles at Greenham Common.

1982 1,691 were arrested at the United Nations.

1982 Nearly a million marched in New York to end the arms race.

1983 777 were arrested at Vandenberg Air Force Base.

1983 1,066 were arrested at Livermore, California.

1983 German Green Party won 27 seats in Parliament.

1983-1990 Pledge of Resistance protested Central America wars.

1983-1993 Witness for Peace groups traveled to Nicaragua.

1984 Winooski 44 sat in and were acquitted by a jury.

1986 Filipinos nonviolently overthrew the Marcos regime.

1987 3,000 protested at Nevada Test site on Mother's Day.

1987-92 Nuremberg Actions blocked weapons trains at Concord.

1987-now ACTUP protested for better AIDS treatment.

1989 Chinese demonstrated for democratic reforms.

1989 Hungary and Poland gained independence.

1989 Czechoslovakia and Bulgaria gained independence.

1990 East and West Germany were reunitied.

1990-1994 Mandela was released and later elected.

1990 Disabled demonstrated in Washington for rights.

1991 Many protested U.S. Gulf War and depleted uranium.

1994 Gorbachev and Strong initiated the Earth Charter.

1996 World Court declared nuclear weapons illegal.

1996-now Roy Bourgeois led protests at Ft. Benning SOA.

1996-now Kelly led Voices in the Wilderness delegations to Iraq.

1999 Protestors disrupted WTO meeting at Seattle.

2000 Yugoslavia replaced Milosevic after election fraud.

2001 Zapatistas marched to Mexico City.

2002 East Timor became independent.

2003 Millions marched to protest imminent U.S.-Iraq war.

2

Liberation from Seven Deadly -Isms

All of us grow up in an environment dominated by our physical surroundings, our family, schools, and culture and are filled with physical, psychological, and social conditioning, which shapes the instincts we inherited through our genes from our ancestors. As we mature and learn how to draw upon the spiritual resources within ourselves to exercise our intuition and freedom of will, we find that we have various tendencies and habits, which may conflict with our spiritual perception of what is best in the situation. To free ourselves from this programming we must learn to acknowledge what it is and make conscious choices based on higher values and careful reasoning. This is not always easy, because the physical and emotional habits may resist our search for wisdom. We call this freeing process liberation—spiritual, theological, political, social, economic, psychological, and physical. To transcend our patterns of conditioning we must become conscious of them by acknowledging and understanding them. The pragmatic test of whether we have become liberated is not only the attitudes we develop and the words we speak but ultimately our behavior and actions, which demonstrate that we are not bound by the old conditioning. However, discussing these issues and changing our attitudes is part of the process of eventually changing our behavior.

Sexism

Because women have had to bear the burden of caring and nurturing children, for generations in evolution and culturally men have taken advantage of their physical strength to dominate women, resulting in the domestic oppression of women and children and in excessive strife and fighting between males. These masculine war-like tendencies are now threatening our entire planet and must be changed. The oppression, dominance, and exploitation of women by men must be stopped. Since these patterns have a long biological, social, economic, and political history, the conditioning is deeply embedded in the culture as well as in the instincts. Our patriarchal society naturally favors men and masculine qualities. These very imbalances have destroyed what could be a natural harmony of cooperation.

To cure a society diseased by domineering and exploitative attitudes and practices we need more women to take a stronger role in politics and culture along with men who are sensitive to the feminine side. We must stop giving over our power to domineering males, and we must not allow them to push us around anymore. We need individuals and groups that are balanced and healthy wholes; we do not necessarily need women who have become over-masculinized and aggressive nor men who have become too weak and passive. Peace and harmony result from equality and justice. Women must assert their right to participate and let their feelings be known, and men must learn to become sensitive to women and their own feelings and intuitions. We need more cooperation and less competition. We need less "leadership" from the top and more group sharing.

As individuals we can examine our daily lives for the vestiges of sexism and work to develop our wholeness. Similarly in groups we can point out to each other how society has been prejudiced against women and work to change our own group attitudes and practices so that feminism has its proper place. Because the old patterns are so ingrained and strong, we must make extra effort to attempt to balance the equation in favor of the side that has been so long oppressed.

Isn't it time we begin to feed and nurture the world and stop trying to arm and dominate it by aggressive force? Can we break the logical chains of rationality that have led us to the development of thermonuclear weapons and star wars? Can we respect the Earth and the beauty of nature instead of plundering and robbing? Can we use art and music to teach and appreciate human values rather than be dominated by science and technology in a mechanized world? Can we learn to share with each other instead of grabbing greedily to possess? Can we supply the world with an abundance of teachers, doctors, and nurses instead of armies, navies, and air forces? We need more women doctors and more male nurses. Can we listen to each other with our hearts instead of making speeches with our egos? The answer to all these questions is yes. In fact, if we do not change our patterns, our very survival is in danger. When we surrender to love of all and follow our hearts, then we will be on the path of healing and happiness.

More feminist awareness will be discussed in the section on "Overcoming Masculine Oppression" under Consensus Decision-making.

Racism

Although physical differences give people an easy means of discrimination, prejudices usually develop for cultural reasons. Different languages and traditions often make communication and understanding difficult. Thus for example, Chinese and Japanese may discriminate against each other's minority populations. Africans in the United States have suffered the worst treatment, because of how they were oppressed as slaves collectively. Native American "Indians" also were badly treated because of cultural differences. In both these latter cases dominating whites often felt insecure and afraid that these people would break out of their oppressed circumstances and fight back or take away the advantages the white settlers had exploited for themselves. Thus racism became wrapped up in economic and social exploitation of a poor class which was easily identifiable so that they could be "kept in their place."

Unfortunately these patterns are still with us, and white people unconsciously consider "colored" peoples as inferior, making it seem permissible to treat them badly, especially those in "foreign" countries. Although whites are in a majority in the industrialized western nations, globally whites are very much in the minority. Thus subconsciously these mostly white nations are afraid of losing control and dominance, as in South Africa where the whites are a small minority. Since the poor tend to have higher birth rates, there is also the fear that the black, brown, and yellow "hordes" will overrun the whites, even in the United States where these minorities are increasing. Maybe non-white peoples historically have larger populations, because culturally they are not as aggressive and warlike.

Perhaps the worst part of racism is how it dehumanizes the racists' own sensitivities toward other human beings. Ironically those who consider others inferior are the ones who have morally and spiritually degraded themselves by their arrogance. They have closed their hearts and minds to souls who are equal to themselves by treating them as objects instead of as spiritual beings. They are violating the fundamental spiritual principle of loving others as ourselves, and not just individually but en masse. We all have the right to choose our friends by affinities, to hire workers by their skill and experience, etc., but to prejudge an entire group of people arbitrarily by skin color or cultural heritage is to limit oneself and commit wholesale injustice.

Foreign policy is often influenced by these racist prejudices in combination with nationalism and imperialism. United States citizens are upset that about 58,000 Americans died in Vietnam, but how many people are concerned that Americans killed at least one million Vietnamese people? Hundreds of thousands may be dying in Africa and tens of thousands in Latin America, and people pay little attention; but if a dozen Europeans or North Americans are killed, it is treated as more important. The United States was a great "melting pot" for Europeans, but now that those who want to come are Latin Americans or Asians, severe restrictions keep most of them out. Black slaves were welcomed, but how many free Africans are allowed?

I personally delight in meeting people from other races and cultures, because I find it very interesting to know a diversity of people. How boring it is when everyone in the group is so much the same! As we develop our global culture and the new civilization of world unity, the intermingling of cultural and racial backgrounds will increase. Intermarriage will become more common, and in the future I prophesy that there will be on Earth a golden race with a great variety of hues and characteristics, all of which will be appreciated for their own beauty.

Imperialism

Nationalism can be either good or bad. In some cases the spirit of nationalism can help to unite people to stand up for their own rights and independence from a foreign power. However, as an independent country grows in nationalism, it tends to become a problem to its neighbors and in abusing its power can become imperialistic and domineering. In the world the smaller countries often need a nationalistic spirit to consolidate their liberation movements and to stand up against the imperialistic influence of powerful nations.

We in the United States have a special responsibility to restrain our government, because since 1945 the USA has established and promoted the Pax Americana for the benefit of the capitalist class and the luxurious lifestyle of North Americans. Two thousand years ago the Romans sent legions of soldiers throughout the Mediterranean world to enforce the Pax Romana. In recent centuries the dominance of the British navy held considerable sway in a Pax Britannica. However, their competing for colonial domination with France, Germany, Italy, and Japan resulted in two world wars and the emergence of the Soviet Union as the predominant power in Eastern Europe and northern Asia, while the United States extended its military forces into Western Europe, Africa, and the Pacific. The western hemisphere had already been marked off as a U.S. preserve by the Monroe Doctrine in 1823.

The Soviet Union became the largest country in the world and attempted to match the military power of the United States in the arms race competition; but the liberalization led by Mikhail Gorbachev allowed Eastern Europe, Afghanistan, and the other Soviet Republics to gain their independence from Russian domination. Their allies in North Korea, Angola, Cuba, and Nicaragua have had to learn how to stand on their own against the threatening military power of the United States. These nations thus have been forced to become non-aligned, independent nations. The non-aligned movement was begun by India's Mahatma Gandhi and Yugoslavia's Tito to give nations the option to join together in freedom from either one of the two dominating superpowers.

After World War II the United States formed a series of alliances with nations whose governments share a common economic ideology, and in this way and by military threats and occasional intervention it attempted to stop the spread of dreaded "Communism." The Soviet Union bore the responsibility for its smaller empire in Eastern Europe, and it also suppressed people's rights and efforts for reform. However, the spread of Gorbachev's *perestroika* (restructuring) and *glasnost* (openness) to Eastern Europe enabled those satellite nations and the Soviet republics to breaking away from Soviet domination. Dogmatic Communism even lost favor in Russia and was abandoned as experimentation with free enterprise expanded.

With the precipitous decline of the Soviet empire and the end of the Cold War, the result is that the United States now has the most powerful navy and air force the world has ever known with military bases throughout most of the world. The governments the U.S. supports are not always the best for the people in those countries, but by the use of military might, which includes military aid as well as sales, conservative and sometimes reactionary and exploitative governments are able to maintain themselves in power by repressing efforts for change in their countries. Now it is time for the United States to give up its domination of other countries and allow true self-determination and freedom without intimidation by the U.S. military and the bribes of U.S. military aid. The people of the world will be freer and small nations can be more independent and self-reliant if they can be liberated from the domination of any superpower and its allies.

Since these alliances are primarily economic and diplomatic, I call this neo-imperialism. The economic aspect can be seen in that the United States, which has about 4.5% of the world population, is using about one-third of the world's resources, and the first world of western

Europe, the U.S., and Japan, which are 20% of the population, are using 80% of the resources. Only 3% of the U.S. military budget actually is used for the defense of U.S. borders. Even the portion that threatened the Soviet Union, supposedly as a deterrent, was much less than the remainder, which directly threatens the third world, as the end of the Cold War has made clear.

No nation has the right to try to force its will on other nations nor to exploit them in selfish ways. How often do we hear politicians talking about the "national interest"? Is this not a group egotism or selfishness? Why not think globally and ask ourselves what is in the best interests of everyone? We must get beyond tribalism and become universal in our loyalties. If we do not begin to think in terms of human unity and the good of the whole Earth, the inevitable struggles between nations could destroy us all. Therefore the nations that try to impose themselves on other countries must be restrained—first by their own citizens and also by people of the world who are considering the good of everyone. Respect for international law, treaties, and world organizations are ways that we can transcend this imperial conflict and call to account the government officials who are acting in a criminal manner through their foreign policies. Nonviolent action to stop these imperialistic designs and crimes may be the most effective way to stimulate the revolutionary changes needed here.

Militarism

The use of military force is the opposite of freedom and respect for self-determination, because it is a violent attempt to force one's will on another. The military is the mindless arm of the state and is sworn to obey its commands. It is like a great machine with many human cogs to operate the technologically sophisticated instruments of killing. In the past warriors used to face other warriors directly and courageously fought face to face. As weapons technology has advanced and killers operate from greater distances, war has become impersonal. Modern wars have also increasingly been waged against civilian populations. Many more civilians were killed in the first world war than ever before, and by the end of the second world war, entire cities were being destroyed from airplanes. Now a nuclear war threatens to kill hundreds of millions, 99% civilians. Even the "low-intensity" wars in the third world attack civilians because of the confusion in fighting insurgent guerrillas. Or, as in the case of the Nicaraguan Contras, economic and civilian targets were hit because of the inability to attack the Sandinista army directly. Thus war has become more devastating, and the military has become more cowardly in hiding behind their sophisticated weapons, while the war-planners and generals sit behind their desks.

Basic training for the military reveals how dehumanizing the military life is, as people are stripped of their individuality and independent thinking skills, natural feelings, and are turned into efficient killing machines programmed to take orders without question. In many nations military service is compulsory. In capitalist societies, such as the United States, the unemployment problem causes the poor and less educated to join the armed forces for the economic security offered. This "poverty draft" insulates the higher classes and educated from the militarism that has been growing steadily in this country.

Militarism is the dominant characteristic of fascism, whether of the right or the left. Power and authority is taken by the leaders of the state, and everyone else is compelled by threats and fear of violence to obey their orders. Independent thinking is discouraged as is the spontaneous expression of feelings. Only in this way can humans be conditioned to kill other humans so easily.

To liberate ourselves from militarism, we must live according to love and respect people as individuals and groups, living freely ourselves according to our own conscience and allowing others the same right. In the way of nonviolence, which attempts to treat everyone with love and understanding, individuals are encouraged to think for themselves and question authority, to learn as much as possible about the issues and share that knowledge with others, both with those who agree and those who do not. Group organization is not usually hierarchical with leaders and authorities above giving orders, but effort is made to treat everyone as on an equal human level. Everyone is encouraged to participate in discussions which result in group decisions. Individuals are free to join or leave groups according to their conscience and interests. By trusting in human freedom to choose and by demonstrating the power of love in action to transform individuals and eventually societies, through nonviolent action we can learn to dissolve the militarism in our society by showing that it is not necessary in order to protect what is good for the whole society. In this way every individual can be empowered, instead of just the leaders at the top.

Materialism

Perhaps the underlying value system that motivates people to develop a militaristic society is materialism. People are afraid of losing their economic security, want to hold on to the wealth that they have accumulated, or are greedy to obtain greater riches. Socrates said that the love of money is the major cause of wars and that the root motivation for the love of money is the desires of the body. A society's desire for luxuries and extra resources, which must be taken from other social groups, causes that society to become feverish and unhealthy. To feed this disease of consuming more than they can produce, the government is obliged to create an extensive military to protect its goods and expand its economic prerogatives in other territories. Thus when justice is lost, the government becomes chaotic until it eventually degenerates into tyranny or fascism, as is described in Plato's *Republic*.

To anyone whose values are spiritual or human, materialism turns everything upside down. When out of selfishness things become more important than people, then spiritual values of truth, love, charity, goodness, wisdom, justice, faith, courage, etc. take a second place to the prevalent "bottom-line" mentality. The bottom line, of course, represents the financial profit to the individual or corporation. When the largeness of that number takes priority over every other consideration, then hedonistic materialism reigns supreme. People will lie, cheat, rob, steal, exploit, manipulate, and sacrifice their other values and their friends and other people for this single-minded objective.

The ironies of this are several. Usually the rich tend to become more caught up in this game, and ironically they are the ones who need more things the least; yet often their lives are unhappier even than the poor they are exploiting, because they are always discontent. The societies with the most luxuries seem to be most obsessed with buying more things. Because of this greed the poor within the society and in other societies do not have enough of even basic needs. In the 1980s while some people were becoming richer, those living in poverty increased in numbers, many more of them young. Living below the poverty line means that a person or family must choose between basic necessities, because their funds are not enough to meet all their needs by that society's standards. Of course the poorest people in the United States would be average members or better in the poorer countries.

Another irony is that the fear and insecurity of this value system causes wealthy nations to spend a tremendous amount of their financial, material, technical, and human resources on the military to defend this way of life. Yet what the military are being paid to do, and all the weapons and equipment they use and stockpile, do not really improve the quality of anyone's life. Of course the salaries these people receive do help them, but this would be the same if they were given the money as welfare. What consumer is benefiting from a Trident submarine or an MX missile or a B2 bomber? Thus the money people are given to spend privately is good for them as well as the economy as a whole, but the work and products that the government obtains by its military spending provide no services to anyone except for this "protection." Do we really need it? Wouldn't everyone in the world be better off if none of the nations had to spend all this effort for fear or aggressive greed? The military industrial complex is the biggest welfare fraud ever! If you don't believe it, check out some of the salaries that are being paid to the engineers, scientists, technicians, and corporate executives. Some of these executives receive millions of dollars per year plus millions more in bonuses! Yet many people think that if a single mother or unemployed person has to go through the humiliation of receiving and using food stamps that this is some sort of abuse.

We need to evaluate our value systems individually as well as collectively and ask ourselves if we are devoting our lives to pleasurable activities and the collection of various toys, or are we giving of our talents and energies for the good of humanity? Can we share some of our possessions to help others and allow ourselves the time to work more for peace and justice? How can one or two people take up a large house when there are so many homeless people among us? Do we buy expensive new clothes when we already have more than we need? Do we need to make so much money that we have to pay federal income tax to a government that is preparing to destroy the world? To live at the maximum income without owing taxes, we are living at the poverty line in solidarity with the poor people of the world and are not contributing to their exploitation and the threats and use of violence in our name. This requires sacrifice of phony values and false needs, but by living communally in order to share goods and limit expenses you may be surprised to find life much more interesting and personally fulfilling.

Dogmatism

Dogma is the Greek word for opinion or decree. Surely we believe that everyone has the right to their own opinions, and even this idea itself is a belief. What happens when people try to force their belief system on someone else? Of course no one can make someone believe something against their will, because belief involves a use of the will. Yet groups often will attempt to manipulate people's beliefs by rewarding and punishing certain attitudes and behaviors. Strong psychological programming will tend to produce individuals and groups who will stubbornly adhere to the dogmas instilled in them. The number of people who think things out for themselves even on major issues is still rather small in our society.

The United States of America was founded on and is supposed to encourage freedom of belief and expression of those beliefs. Yet religious beliefs can prove as resistant to reason and change as the nationalistic ideologies promoted by governments. The Soviet Union was more controlled in its expression of ideas until it was opened up with *glasnost*. For example, in the USSR it was illegal to advocate war and other anti-social behavior. In the United States we are permitted to advocate anything except the violent overthrow of the government. I believe in as much freedom of ideas as possible so that people can learn from the free exchange, because I trust that if all ideas are allowed, people will eventually choose the best. We need not be ruled by fear of bad ideas, because we can show their deficiencies and replace them with better concepts.

The problems occur when people act upon their dogmas without intelligently thinking out their consequences. People tend to act based on their belief systems. If this results, either intentionally or unintentionally, in injustice, then the conflict must be resolved. People who are psychologically insecure will tend to cling to their beliefs and not want to question them. Thus the combination of religious fundamentalism and nationalistic patriotism, which are often thoroughly instilled in people through the family, church, schools, and the media can lead to a blindness that supports U.S. policies and hates anything vaguely referred to as Communist. In the United States and much of Latin America this fear of Communism was so extreme and irrational that as a collective neurosis it resulted in very unhealthy attitudes and governmental policies. Anti-Communism tended to be irrational, because of dogma based on false propaganda and immense distortion of what Communism is and what the real intentions of Communist governments are. This red-baiting is used by politicians to manipulate voters, discredit reformers, and justify immoral policies.

Yet we all believe in something, because all our conscious actions come from some motivation and objective we believe is possible to attain. We need to evaluate our own beliefs to see if the values implicit in them are really for the best of everyone. Also if we have faith that our beliefs are good, then we do not need to try to force them on people by military power, but we can allow a free process of discussion in which everyone has the right to participate.

So what do we do when a group or government tries to force its dogmatic beliefs on other people by force of arms or unfair discrimination? Some of the beliefs in the United States that tend to prevent reform are that there is a free marketplace of ideas, a free political system, guarantees of free speech, press, and religion, and open attitudes; but we find that the reality is that money interests dominate that marketplace, that political system, the major media and churches, and that the attitudes of most Americans tend to be closed because of so many other superficial interests. In one sense we need the faith that we can change these processes by free discussion, but on the other hand this blind belief in symbolic efforts may prevent us from taking the nonviolent action necessary to stimulate the changes needed in this planetary emergency. The governments are acting with millions of people and hundreds of billions of dollars to enforce their beliefs throughout the world. If these actions are ethically wrong and harmful to people, we have a moral obligation not only to express our beliefs symbolically, but I believe we also have a conscientious duty, if we feel called to it, to act in loving ways to stop these terrible crimes.

When people do act on opposing belief systems, then there will be conflict. Yet by confrontation of opposing views differences in worldviews can be resolved. If our belief is in love and nonviolence as the basis for our action, then this confrontation will be what Martin Luther King called "creative conflict." In other words when people are active yet nonviolent the process of change will tend to be promoted but at the same time be less destructive, thus creative. We should realize that nonviolent action is based on beliefs and values; but at the same time as it stimulates people to choose more consciously what they are supporting, it does not use violent force against people. Rather nonviolent activists present their bodies and lives in the way of harmful actions, willing to take on suffering if it is inflicted by the opponent without retaliating. Thus not only are beliefs symbolically challenged, but the behaviors that result from them are also physically challenged without forcing the new belief on them. Yet the new beliefs and values are presented to those whose behaviors are being protested in a way that they cannot ignore. When the ignorance in our society is so great that it is threatening the entire human race and mother Earth, then it seems to me we must experiment with such bold moves.

Egotism

Ego is the Greek word for I. Every personality has an ego and could not exist without one. Egotism, however, is the inflation of this personal self beyond its useful function. Thus sometimes we need to practice "egopuncture" to deflate our own sense of personal importance when it gets in the way of other people's interests and expressions.

Although part of our liberation is personal empowerment, it needs to be blended with group empowerment and global thinking. The process of being true to our self and manifesting our integrity is subtly different from aggrandizing our personality and certainly is not dominating others. This respect for the true self within us must include the self within others or else we find ourselves in the double standard of egotism, which implies that I am more important, better, or worth more than you. As Brian Willson said of the people in Central America, "We are not worth more; they are not worth less." By respecting equality of persons we are not only empowering others but in a spiritual way are empowering our own true self.

Egotism is especially noticeable in small groups, because the dominant personality tends to restrain the opportunities of others. The group where individuals are able to see beyond their own personal considerations in order to harmonize these with others' interests will be an empowered group that will flow and change and operate as an organic whole rather than be pulled and pushed in different directions haphazardly.

Egos of different sizes and temperaments can be equally problematic. We tend to think of the big ego as always being inflictive, but it can also be supportive and capable of taking on large responsibilities if the group so chooses to allow this. The person with a large ego can strengthen the group but must be very careful not to dominate and take over. The smaller ego also may be supportive and capable of accomplishing much if others are supportive of that person. However, the small ego that is insecure can pull energy from the group by acting helpless and always seeking emotional approval. The group can help this type of person become weaned from dependency by letting the person gain maturity through experience. People in the group also need to keep the strong ego from dominating the process and point out the need for restraint when appropriate.

As our groups become successful, we need to be careful of group egotism in relation to other groups and the public. Again self-esteem is not the same as conceit which comes out of self-deception. If groups are unable to cooperate with other groups working for similar goals, then the coalition building needed to develop a large movement becomes problematic. Similarly if we act toward our adversary as though we are somehow morally superior beings, then our self-righteousness is sure to bring a negative reaction. We can believe in ourselves and our cause, but we must also believe in the true selves of all other individuals, realizing that they too understand some truths. If we listen to them as equals, they are likely to reciprocate; and both of us are likely to learn and gain from the experience. By understanding others' viewpoints we learn how to communicate more effectively with them.

The subtleties of egotism will always be with us, because we are always attempting to harmonize our personal interests and responsibilities with those of other individuals and groups. If we do not look out for our own interests, then who will? As long as we have a body, we must take care of it and keep it functioning. No one is likely to know our hurts and joys if we do not tell anyone. At the same time we need to observe and listen to others so that we can best relate with their situations.

So from the immense world problems we face, as we begin to work on solving them, we find that peace must begin within ourselves. If we are to become effective peacemakers and really change the world, we have to work on ourselves first and while we are in the process of developing group efforts for social change. To ignore our personal development for the sake of the world is to reduce our personal effectiveness in working for change; but to ignore the world to concentrate on our own spiritual growth is to limit that to a selfish and narcissistic process. Thus we must work simultaneously on transforming ourselves and our society; and as we shall see, each process helps the other.

3

Group Process

Affinity Groups

An affinity group (AG) is usually composed of 5-20 people who have been brought together by some common experience. In addition to concerns for peace and justice, they may be from the same community, church, local peace group, have a similar political perspective, a common cause such as feminism, anarchism, nonviolence as a way of life, etc., or they may form out of a nonviolence training or to employ a similar tactic at a direct action. Affinity groups are the basic decision-making bodies of the action.

Affinity groups serve as a source of support and solidarity for their members. Feelings of being isolated or alienated from the movement, crowd, or the world in general can be alleviated through the friendship and trust which develops when an affinity group works, plays, and relates together over a period of time. Everyone participating in any action is encouraged to join or form an affinity group. Individuals can come to a nonviolence training on their own initiative and there find like-minded people who can then form an affinity group. Others may work in groups for weeks or longer, becoming a close-knit family of activists. Individuals may also join an already established affinity group for a particular action. By having these groups, it makes it much more difficult for outside provocateurs to go unnoticed.

The name of these units comes from the "grupos de affinidad" of the anarchist movement in Spain in the early part of the 20th century. Each affinity group is encouraged to choose a name for identification and may wish to have similar T-shirts or arm bands. The more affinity groups can meet and work together, the closer will be the personal relationships and the group cohesion and effectiveness. At least one group meeting is needed before the action, which may be after the nonviolence training, in order to discuss legal and jail preparation and allow time to explore everyone's questions, fears, reactions, emotions, and attitudes in depth. The more prepared affinity groups are before the action, the better it is likely to go.

Most affinity groups choose to operate with consensus decision-making in order to establish certain principles of unity for the group. For example, each affinity group should discuss and agree to the nonviolence discipline for the action. If there is a disagreement, a spokesperson for the group should contact the organizers of the action or the spokes-council in order to resolve it. Individuals who have difficulty consenting to the principles of a particular affinity group may find that they have more affinity with another group.

* *

Christians do not quarrel with anyone,
do not attack anyone nor use violence against anyone;
on the contrary,
they themselves without murmuring bear violence;
but by this very relation to violence
they not only free themselves,
but also the world from external power.
Leo Tolstoy

* *

Roles in the Affinity Group

Specific roles may be taken on by different members of each affinity group. Each role serves a function that is important to the whole group and the action. These roles may be rotated from time to time; e.g., the same person should not always be the spokesperson for the group.

* The **spokesperson** represents the decisions and concerns of the AG to the larger council of spokes, listens carefully and takes notes at the council meetings, and then reports back the council's decisions, proposals, and concerns to the group.

* The **contact person** maintains an up-to-date list of the AG members' names, addresses and phones, and communicates with the organizers of the action.

* The **legal spokesperson** communicates with the legal collective or with lawyers and those knowledgeable on the legal issues and attempts to find answers to AG members' legal questions and concerns. The legal spoke may also communicate legal strategies to and from other AG's legal spokes.

* The **media spokesperson** is responsible for meeting with the press and radio or TV reporters to give information according to the wishes of individual members of the AG. Media spokes may meet together as a media collective and coordinate publicity for an action, give out press releases, call a press conference, etc.

* **Peacekeepers** are responsible for watching the emotional tone of the action and when noticing persons getting upset should calmly approach and sensitively attempt to assist people in resolving their conflicts and concerns. At a demonstration peacekeepers may gently keep people informed as to the legal areas of protest and serve as a mediator between law enforcement officers and the protestors in keeping the demonstration orderly. If there is a counter-demonstration, peacekeepers may

serve as buffers between the opposing protestors. If violence begins to break out, it is the responsibility of peacekeepers to intervene nonviolently and calm the situation. Actually in such an emergency every participant in a nonviolent action should act as a peacekeeper.
* A **medic** with basic skills and a first-aid kit can be helpful.

At the time of the action, the affinity group will be divided into two parts: those choosing to risk arrest and the others who serve as support people. Both are important functions essential to the action. In the case of those risking arrest the sacrifices are fairly obvious, but good support will enable the action to be successful and will encourage, instead of discourage, future actions.

Those risking arrest should consider the following:
* Discuss possible tactics before the action, coordinate with other AGs, make or revise decisions during the action.
* Discuss legal options and strategies, attempt to reach consensus on solidarity issues, such as not paying bail, not signing a cite release, not paying fines, not accepting probation, etc., as well as discussing who will plead not guilty and go to trial.
* Make personal preparations, set time commitments, clear outstanding warrants (such as unpaid traffic tickets) to avoid additional charges and to avoid complicating jail solidarity.

Support people may serve in the following ways:
Before the action:
* List all members of the group and the personal needs of each person who may be arrested:
-name, address, key phone numbers, and birth-date.

-expected legal strategy (e.g. plea, noncooperation)
-health and medical requirements (contact lenses).
-a lawyer, if the person wants one.
-telephone calls to relatives, employers, friends.
-child care responsibilities.
-household chores (feeding pets, watering plants).
-bills to be paid.
-deadline by which bail may need to be paid.
-personal possessions to be left behind (car keys, vehicle license number, wallet, etc.) Mark with AG name or personal name.
* Make sure the group has enough resources for the action: food, money, vehicles, people filling different roles, telephone access. Discuss possible emergencies.
* Handle car keys and house keys, glasses, contact lens supplies, prescription medications, paperback books, cash, etc.
* Provide hugs and quality time to discuss the decision to risk arrest and arrange when you can be called collect from jail.
* Give your name, information, and how long you will be available for support work to central support or the jail collective.

At the time of the action:
* Provide transportation to the action site, water, food, hugs, and cheers.
* Be ready to receive hugs, last minute unloading of possessions, and information as to where those arrested are likely to be taken.
* Know the boundaries of arrest and non-arrest areas.
* Serve as a legal observer during the arrest situation by taking pictures, video, or notes for possible use as evidence in court.

After the arrest:
* Notify people as requested by the one arrested.
* Provide jail support as requested (bring medications, lens supplies, books, money for commissary account, visitation).
* Send letters and newspaper clippings.
* Keep action organizers updated as to the status of individuals.
* Attend and bring friends to court arraignment and trial to show public support for the action.
* Pay emergency bail if requested.

When people are released from jail:
* Provide hugs and kisses, decent munchies, transportation home, and quality time to discuss the experience.

Consensus Decision-making

Consensus is a decision-making process that reflects commitment to the right of every person to influence decisions that affect them. Consensus comes to us through the Quakers, but it has been used by tribal cultures since prehistory. The Six Nations of the Iroquois, for example, use their own form of consensus government to this day. Children also use an informal consensus process as they make up games, choose roles, and play together.

Consensus is a creative process. It is a process for synthesizing the ideas and concerns of all group members. Unlike voting, it is not an adversary, win/lose method. With consensus, we do not have to choose between two alternatives. Instead we can create a third, a fourth or more as we see that problems may have many possible solutions. Those who hold views different from ours do not become opponents; instead, their views can be seen as giving us a fresh and valuable perspective. As we work to meet their concerns, our proposals may be strengthened. When we use consensus, we encourage each person's active participation, and we listen carefully to what each person says.

Consensus is not the same as a vote. It does not necessarily mean total agreement. Consensus does not mean that everyone thinks that the decision made is necessarily the best one possible, or even that they are sure it will work. What it does mean is that in coming to that decision, no one felt that their position on the matter was misunderstood or that it was not given a proper hearing. It also means that the final decision does not violate anyone's fundamental moral values; for if it did, they would be obligated to block consensus or leave the group.

During discussion the issues will tend to emerge into a proposal for the group to implement. Once the proposal has been formulated, clarifying questions may precede the discussion as to its merits. The procedure is that discussion must focus on the proposal before the group until it has been withdrawn or gained consent. During the discussion concerns and modifications may be raised which may amend the proposal. Such friendly amendments must be acceptable to the originator of the proposal. If people decide that the proposal is not appropriate, it may be withdrawn or dropped. After adequate discussion, the facilitator may begin to test for consensus by asking if there are any concerns or reservations. If there are none, then silence or the twinkling of fingers or nodding of heads may indicate consensus. If anyone feels any qualms about it, it is their responsibility to voice them so that they can be heard by the group and discussed. Often reservations may lead to modifications of the proposal so that it is still acceptable to everyone. If a substantial number of people have reservations, then the proposal is usually dropped.

If a single person or a small percentage of the whole group still have reservations unresolved by the discussion, then they have the following choices:

* **Non-support** – "I don't like it, but I can live with it."
* **Standing aside** – "I personally won't do this; but I won't stop others from doing it, and I'll stay in the group."
* **Blocking** – "I cannot allow the group to do this, because I believe it would be morally wrong to do so. I'm going to stay in the group and try to persuade you this is wrong." Consensus has been blocked, and the proposal is dropped.
* **Withdrawing** – "I no longer share the values and unifying principles of this group. Therefore I am leaving the group." (In the rare case where a person may try to block a group from fulfilling its main objectives, the other members of the group could decide to withdraw themselves from that person who apparently is an agent provocateur.)

In the case of a block, the proposal is dropped or reworked to satisfy the persons who are blocking. In the larger sense in direct action protests we are saying to our society, "You do not have our consent to perpetrate these wrongs. We believe it is morally wrong and are acting to block nonviolently those wrongs from occurring."

When there are people not supporting or standing aside, it is referred to as a luke-warm consensus, which is like a luke-warm drink or a luke-warm bath in that it may be better than nothing but hardly ideal.

Thus the proposal goes through a synthesis process in which everyone has a chance to express feelings and concerns. Consensus is based on the belief that people can talk peacefully about their differences and reach a mutually satisfactory position. When consensus is used well, it empowers individuals, because the process constantly affirms the value of each person's rare experience. It often brings out our best insights and encourages our sense of responsibility.

Once a decision is made, it is important to make sure that how it is going to implemented has also been decided. What the decision is may be repeated and recorded in the notes of the meeting.

Review of Consensus Procedure:
* Problem stated: What are we talking about?
* Question clarified: What needs to be decided?
* Discussion: What are all the views?
* Proposal made: What action will the group take?
* Proposal discussed: clarifying questions, good points, concerns.
* Proposal modified by friendly amendments or withdrawn.
* Test for consensus:
* Restate proposal.
* Call for concerns and objections.
* Attempt to synthesize objections into the proposal.
* If decision is blocked, proposal is dropped.
* If consensus is reached, show visual or verbal agreement.
* Assign tasks to implement the decision.

Roles in a Consensus Meeting
* The **facilitator or co-facilitators** help the group define decisions that need to be made, prioritize the agenda, make sure the necessary roles are filled, call on people to speak in turn while encouraging reticent speakers, may suggest ways to discuss issues by items or with techniques such as brain-storming, small group discussion, go-rounds where everyone speaks, etc., and generally keep the meeting focused and moving through the decision-making stages. The facilitator should remain

neutral on the topics discussed. If the person who is facilitating wishes to enter the discussion it should be clear they are temporarily dropping the role of facilitator. The facilitator should make sure that proposals are clearly understood by restating them and calling for clarifying questions prior to discussion. The facilitator should call on people in order unless someone hasn't spoken at all while others have spoken several times; or when someone has a process question or suggestion, they may raise both hands and be called on immediately.

* The **timekeeper** warns the group halfway through and at the end of each time period allotted to agenda items. At the end of the time period, the group may decide to allot more time or go on to the next agenda item.

* The **note-taker** records minutes, taking special care to write down each decision the group makes and to note who is responsible for carrying it out. They may also take on the responsibility of sending out the minutes to the members after the meeting.

* The **vibes-watcher** has been referred to as having an underview of the meeting. Vibes-watchers observe the body language, the undercurrent of feelings and tension, and at appropriate moments may recommend that the group pause to breathe deeply or stretch or take a break or sing a song, or even acknowledge their feelings. A song or non-competitive game can be used as a "light and lively" to help the group relax and refresh.

* Spokes-councils may be held during an action in which several affinity groups participate. Each AG sends a spokesperson to the council for overall decision-making. If the spokes have been empowered to make a decision for their group, the council may then make a consensus decision for the whole action. Or proposals may go from the council back to the affinity groups for ratification. If all the AGs consent and send back spokes saying so, then

consensus is reached. At spokescouncil meetings usually only spokes are allowed to speak, but interested members of AGs may sit behind the circle of spokes and pass notes or whisper to their spoke. This is sometimes referred to as the jail model spokescouncil.

Meeting Procedure

* Connect by sitting down, singing, breathing together, praying or meditating, etc.
* Choose a facilitator, note-taker, timekeeper, and vibes-watcher.
* Introductions or basic check-ins of how people are feeling.
* Collect items for the agenda; set times, prioritize; or review agenda.
* Go through agenda as agreed upon, taking breaks as appropriate.
* Collect names, addresses, and phones if needed.
* Set a date, time, and place for the next meeting.
* Announcements.
* Evaluate meeting.
* Closing circle.

Attitudes and Behaviors which Help Consensus

* **Responsibility** - Participants are responsible for voicing their opinions, participating in the discussion, and implementing the agreements.
* **Self-discipline** - Refrain from talking too much, repeating what has already been said, or interrupting. Listen carefully and think before speaking. Allow pauses after each person speaks.
* **Respect** - Respect everyone and trust them to make responsible contributions.
* **Cooperation** - Look for areas of agreement for common ground and build on them. Avoid competitive right/wrong, win/lose thinking.

* **Struggle** - Use clear means of disagreement, not put-downs. Use disagreements and arguments to grow and change. Work hard to build unity in the group, but not at the expense of members.

Overcoming Discrimination

Hidden Assumptions and Attitudes:
1. The assumption that the dominant group represents humanity as a whole: for example, that "man" refers to all people, that pink band-aids are flesh-colored.
2. The assumption that we all share common experiences, resources, and interests. Women's experience is different from men's, blacks' from that of whites', working-class people's from middle-class people's. Society's institutions treat us differently and we grow up with different expectations and opportunities. We do not have the same access to money and time or to resources such as transportation and emotional support. We have different responsibilities and different limitations. As we work together, we need to bear this in mind.
3. The assumption that discrimination does not hurt the dominant group. Restrictive sex roles hurt men as well as women. Racism hurts us all. Both divide us as potential friends and allies.
4. The assumption that education on these issues should be carried out by the oppressed—that people of color should educate white people, that women should raise the consciousness of men. Yet no one can raise someone else's consciousness—that is a task we each must take for ourselves. Because change benefits us all, it is up to each of us to learn about and raise issues other than our own.

5. The assumption that the values, symbols, and world-view of the dominant culture are universal.

6. The assumption that people from different groups and lifestyles should try to look and act like members of the dominant group, or should fit the stereotypes to make dominant group members feel comfortable.

7. The assumption that these issues of liberation and survival are side issues that distract from the real work and can be conveniently set aside whenever they make people uncomfortable.

Ways We Can Work for Change:

1. Raise the issues of racism, sexism, classism, heterosexism, ageism, discrimination against the disabled, etc. Speak up about them. Make them our concern.

2. Join together with people of our own sex, class, or race to share experiences, frustrations, pain, and develop common understandings. Make time for consciousness raising.

3. Educate ourselves about people who are different from us. Read the writings of people of color, working-class people, women, etc. Learn the history of Africa, the Americas, Polynesia, Asia. Learn other languages.

4. Tell our own personal histories to each other. Recognize that we are all ethnic, that we are rich in the diversity of our heritages and life experiences.

5. Realize that third-world people face daily threats which are more immediate than what we experience in a wealthy country.

6. Understand that many peace and justice issues affect third-world communities in special ways. For example:

Nuclear programs are dependent on uranium mined in southern Africa and on native lands in the U.S., Canada, Australia, etc.

Military intervention is planned to prevent self-determination throughout the third world.

Military recruiting is targeted at areas of high unemployment. With few jobs available, African-Americans and Latinos often have little choice but to enlist.

The massive transfer of resources to the military in recent budgets has particularly hurt the poor.

The massive expenditures for arms worldwide take funds and resources needed for economic development.

7. Learn and act upon issues of special concern to third-world communities. Integrate the concerns of these communities in your approach to peace issues.

8. Develop working relationships with all groups involved with social change, including African-American, Latino, Asian, and native groups. In planning for events form coalitions early, which include as many groups as possible.

9. Do not force your agenda on other organizations.

Overcoming Masculine Oppression

Many of the problems found in anti-war groups are those of domination within the movement. People join a social change movement in order to alleviate an external problem. Too often we are confronted with the same kind of behavior we find in our daily lives. We are all too often stifled by heavy-handed authority—parents or spouse at home, teachers at school, bosses at work.

People want not only to be accepted in these groups but also to make a contribution and be active participants. In order to work successfully to change things, we must also pay attention to our own behavior. More often than not, men are the ones dominating group activity. Such behavior is therefore termed a "masculine behavior pattern" not because women never act that way, but because it is generally men who do it.

Specific ways we can be responsible in groups:

* Not interrupting people who are speaking. We can even leave space after each speaker, counting to five before speaking.

* Becoming a good listener. Good listening is as important as good speaking. It is important not to withdraw when not speaking; good listening is active participation.

* Getting and giving support. We can help each other be aware of and point out patterns of domination, as well as affirm each other as we move away from those ways. It is important that men support and challenge each other, rather than asking women to do so. This will also allow women more space to break out of their own conditioned role of looking after men's needs while ignoring their own.

* Not giving answers and solutions. We can give our opinions in a manner which says we believe our ideas valuable, but not more important than others' ideas.

* Relaxing. The group will do fine without our anxiety attacks.

* Not speaking on every subject. We need not share every idea we have, at least not with the whole group.

* Not putting others down. We need to check ourselves when we are about to attack or "one-up" another. We can ask ourselves, "Why am I doing this? What am I feeling? What do I need?"

Common problems to be aware of:

* Hogging the show. Talking too much, too long and too loud.

* Problem solver. Continually giving the answer or solution before others have had much chance to contribute.

* Speaking in capital letters. Giving one's own solutions or opinions as the final word on the subject, often aggravated by tone of voice and body posture.

* Defensiveness. Responding to every contrary opinion as though it were a personal attack.
* Nit-picking. Pointing out minor flaws in statements of others and stating the exception to every generality.
* Restating. Especially what has just been said by a non-dominant person.
* Attention seeking. Using all sorts of dramatics to get the spotlight.
* Task and content focus. To the exclusion of nurturing individuals or the group through attention to process and form.
* Put-downs and one-upmanship. "I used to believe that, but now ..." or "How can you possibly say that?"
* Negativism. Finding something wrong or problematical in everything.
* Focus transfer. Transferring the focus of the discussion to one's own pet raps.
* Residual office holder. Hanging on to formal powerful positions.
* Self-listening. Formulating a response after the first few sentences, not listening to anything from that point on and leaping in at the first pause.
* Inflexibility and dogmatism. Taking a last stand for one's position on even minor items.
* Avoiding feelings. Intellectualizing, withdrawing into passivity or making jokes when it's time to share personal feelings.
* Condescension and paternalism. "Now, do any women have anything to add?"
* Being "on the make." Using sexuality to manipulate people.
* Seeking attention and support from women while competing with men.
* Running the show. Continually taking charge of tasks before others have a chance to volunteer.

* Pack-ratitis. Protectively storing key group information for one's own use and benefit.
* Speaking for others. "A lot of us think that we should ..." or "What so-and-so really meant was ..."

The full wealth of knowledge and skill is severely limited by such behavior. Women and men who don't feel comfortable participating in a competitive atmosphere are, in effect, cut off from the interchange of experience and ideas.

If sexism and domineering egotism is not ended within social-change groups, it is not a movement for real social change. The movement would flounder amidst divisiveness, and sex oppression would go on. Thus we must work to free women and men from oppressive sex role conditioning and from subtle as well as blatant forms of male supremacy.

* *

Do not do to others what you would not want them to do to you.
Confucius
* *

Hate is never conquered by hate;
hate is conquered by love.
This is an eternal law.
Dhammapada
* *

4

Creative Actions

We can act creatively in many different ways in working toward our goals of peace and justice. Getting arrested is usually a last resort after all other efforts have failed to bring about a needed change. Most of the methods involve communication and education. In most everyday situations we usually correct problems ourselves, or we tell someone who is able to do what needs to be done. If they agree, the problem can be easily solved. If there is not agreement, one avenue is to appeal to a higher authority, usually that person's supervisor or in the judicial system a higher court. Only when there is a consistent pattern running through the whole system of corruption or intransigence to fair human values is it necessary to mount a nonviolence campaign.

Investigation and Research

The first stage of a nonviolent campaign is learning about the problem that needs correcting by studying its history, politics, economics, sociology, and psychology. This means answering such questions as:

Who has been doing what to whom?
Who is in control and wielding the power or making the decisions?
How are financial incentives and economic relations affecting this?
What social relationships and cultural traditions are involved?
Why are people acting as they are?

What is motivating them?
And how can they be given alternative options that are best for all?

The investigation can be done by observing, talking to people, and by direct experience in the situation. Research can be through studying books and periodicals, seeing and hearing news reports, and by searching the world wide web. This first stage is sometimes known as "doing your homework" so that you are informed of the circumstances and will not make a fool out of yourself. Of course not every person participating in a nonviolent campaign has to do all the research. Information can be shared, and often those who enter a campaign in the later and more urgent stages find that they are joining a group effort that has its own history of investigation and research. However, these efforts always need to be updated as circumstances change.

Negotiation or Arbitration

The second stage is approaching the adversary in order to negotiate a mutually agreeable solution. Sometimes this process can be assisted by a neutral mediator, and in some cases both sides may agree to accept the decision of an arbitrator. Good communication skills and open friendliness are especially helpful in achieving a negotiated settlement. A good listener will be able to see the other person's point of view as if it is one's own, and a good speaker will help the listener see one's own view also. This is one of the most important stages in peace-making. One of the main problems about George W. Bush is that he has a tendency to go by his gut instincts, and he often refuses to consider negotiating at all. If the problem can not be worked out directly and you still believe that you are right and that your adversary is being unfair, then one has the right to appeal to others and the general public by means of communication and education.

Public Education on the Issue

Consciousness can be raised on an issue by making speeches to people, holding discussions, writing letters, going to the media for interviews on radio or television, publishing information on a website, printing leaflets, flyers, pamphlets, and books, etc. The creative arts can also be very effective in getting one's message across by creating pictorial art, composing songs, doing street theater or public plays, making educational films or videos, and so on. Leaflets can be handed out to the adversaries and involved persons as well as to the general public. Education can be promoted by organizing teach-ins in classes, churches, civic clubs or for any group of people or wherever people are gathered. If these efforts are not successful, they can be enhanced by greater persistence using more overt tactics such as picketing. Such efforts are a transition to the next stage of holding demonstrations, rallies, marches, and vigils.

Vigils and Demonstrations

These involve more people and more of their time being involved but demonstrate the deep concern that they feel. A person holding a sign for an hour or more is saying much more than what is written on the sign. They are essentially pleading with people to take this message seriously. Obviously the more people that are involved in these activities the greater the effect will be. This is where a successful nonviolence campaign uses real people power. If hundreds or thousands of people care enough about an issue to come out in their spare time to march or demonstrate, that sends a strong message to those in control of the issue that they want to see a change.

Everyone has the right to express their views on moral and political issues, and thanks to the first amendment to the *United States Constitution*, people in this country are supposed to be able to do it without being treated as criminals. To change the immoral policies of our government it is essential that as many people as possible express their concern and disapproval as actively as they can.

All people are encouraged to gather in groups and indicate their moral outrage at the genocidal and suicidal policies of a nuclear weapons super-power developing first-strike weapons and ballistic missile defense in order to attain world domination by military power. These gatherings and rallies may be as often and in as many places as people wish to hold them. People can hold signs and banners, pray or meditate, sing or chant, and make their presence known to the authorities who are perpetrating these atrocities.

For those who do not wish to risk arrest by law enforcement authorities, there are many ways to express one's views and try to influence the government and other citizens to change these policies. Whenever demonstrations are held at military bases or governmental institutions, individuals can always feel welcome to attend to indicate their concern without much danger of being arrested by mistake. There is always some chance that a few individuals can be swept up along with others even though they had no intention of challenging the legality of these policies. However, in such instances the charges are usually dropped, or those individuals are acquitted after a trial.

Boycotts and Strikes

If even these demonstrations are not enough, then those in the campaign may deny themselves certain products or services in boycotts and can take off from work or school in a strike. These tactics are designed to use an economic leverage to reach those who may be oblivious to reason and justice. These can be especially effective when dealing with greedy corporations or companies. In the 19th century abolitionists boycotted products made by slave labor such as cotton and sugar. In the 1960s and 1970s the United Farm Workers led by Cesar Chavez asked people to boycott grapes. The international campaign of divestment from South Africa eventually helped bring an end to apartheid. Many people now currently boycott products that are made by "sweat-shop" labor exploitation, and students have been trying to stop their universities from conducting military research or sponsoring military officer training for many years. Many of the most egregious corporations have been targeted by activists. Often these commercial pressures can help these businesses "convert" to more beneficial products or to treating their workers better.

Legal Suits and Noncooperation

If one has enough money for a lawyer and believes one has a good legal case, one may take the opponent to court. If a moral issue does not have a legal justification, or if one is challenging the immoral policies of a government that is not likely to be reigned in by its own courts, then one may proceed to the next step of noncooperation. Mahatma Gandhi said that not cooperating with evil is as much a duty as cooperating with good. In the case of a government, this may mean not paying taxes just as many in the thirteen colonies refused to pay taxes to

England when they believed they were not being democratically represented. Noncooperation adds onto boycotts and strikes by refusing to cooperate with activities that one believes are part of the evil. For example, in the 1950s Dorothy Day and Catholic Workers in New York City refused to take shelter as instructed during air raid drills that were designed to prepare people for a nuclear war. When a small group of tyrants or foreign invaders are trying to impose their will on a country, massive noncooperation can make it impossible for them to govern. Gene Sharp and others have argued that a society educated and disciplined in nonviolent action could effectively defend its rights against any militaristic attempt to "conquer" them, thus making weapons and the military obsolete.

Civil Disobedience

Finally if all else has failed to remove the evil, one may even sacrifice one's freedom by placing oneself in the way of the evil action in some way and then refuse to cooperate when law enforcement officers order one to move. This may be done in various ways by trespassing where one is prohibited or by refusing to leave a public or private place when ordered to do so. This type of disobedience is called civil, because it is done peacefully and openly in a civil manner. Further steps of noncooperation may involve not walking when arrested. In a nonviolence campaign these are considered the last resort, because we do not believe in hurting other people. Those who do not believe in the power of nonviolence, of course, often resort to injuring others or even killing them. For those in the nonviolence movement a gray area is damaging property. Most believe that damaging private property or public property is a violation and should be avoided. However, some in the plowshares movement have argued that destroying a weapon of destruction is not wrong, because it has no "proper" use and thus is not "property." Yet in a large demonstration even a few individuals damaging property and looting can greatly diminish the integrity of the cause.

Fasting

Even in jail and also while not imprisoned, a person may demonstrate a deep appeal by fasting. A juice fast is relatively safe usually for several weeks; but a fast on water may endanger one's health and life after a few days, though many have gone as long as forty days or more without experiencing serious harm. Beyond that on only water one can expect to have stomach damage, organs failing, blindness, and finally death. Fasting without even water is even more drastic and can bring serious injury and death within a few days. Thus fasting can be a dangerous form of appeal. During the Vietnam War some Buddhists in Vietnam and some Americans in the United States committed suicide as a protest by pouring gasoline on themselves and striking a match. Most people in the peace movement value life very much and are horrified by such sacrifices; yet each individual must act according to one's own conscience.

Constructive Activity

Working for peace and justice are positive activities, and it is important not to get too caught up in the negative aspect of protesting against the violations of these ideals. For our personal health and the welfare of our community we need to spend most of our time on the constructive activities that make life work well. This will also help observers who otherwise might perceive nonviolent activists as too negative, always being against things but never building anything positive. Many have found that by living and working in communities with people of similar values these goals can much more easily be attained. Everyone who can needs to do something to contribute to the world.

Mahatma Gandhi emphasized the importance of what he called the constructive program. He observed that British mercantilism was exploiting India by taking their raw materials and natural resources to England for manufacturing into clothing and other products, which were then shipped back to India for great profits. So Gandhi began a campaign to encourage Indians to spin their own cloth and encouraged people to wear only "home-spun" *(khadi)*. Gandhi himself spent a certain amount of time spinning every day. Home-spun clothes became the emblem of Indian independence, and the spinning wheel a symbol of the new nation. Many peace activists such as Koinonia in Georgia have formed communal farms to grow food and market it. Those in the resistance community at Jonah House in Baltimore often worked painting houses so that they could be free to protest and go to prison in between jobs. They also distributed donated food to the poor. Many Catholic Worker houses spend most of their time helping the poor in many ways. Others have started schools to teach the ways of peace at all levels. Some have formed cooperative publishing companies or produced a regular newspaper or magazine. As the Buddha taught long ago, right livelihood is an important fundamental.

A nonviolent revolution is not a program of seizure of power.
It is a program of transformation of relationships
ending in a peaceful transfer of power.
Mahatma Gandhi

Individual Conscience

These stages of a nonviolent campaign should not be taken to mean that the latter stages are more important or a stronger protest. They may or may not be. Each individual needs to search within oneself to see how best one can contribute to making this world a better place. This often depends on what kind of abilities a person has and what they feel right about doing. A skilled investigator or researcher can contribute immensely to improving society and may never demonstrate or get arrested. An artist or playwright or musician may create in ways that lift others to new heights of awareness. Teachers have obvious gifts in this field. A good business person may find successful ways to communicate and educate or may contribute money to support the efforts of others. A skilled lawyer is usually a tremendous asset to a nonviolence campaign in many ways. Doctors and nurses are needed to care for people who may be injured by police brutality or who may even be too poor to afford medical treatment because of their dedication to social reforms.

5

Legal Process

Nuremberg Actions or Civil Disobedience

Many people in the peace movement believe that our society is facing a serious crisis with the endless war on terrorism declared by President George W. Bush and his stated intention to go to war against other nations he calls evil, because they are attempting to obtain nuclear weapons. The hypocrisy of this policy is rather obvious when one reaizes that the United States has more nuclear weapons than any other country by far with the lone exception of Russia, which has been greatly weakened and has reduced its military power. Because of the overwhelming horror of the danger of a nuclear war and this oppressive police state we are facing daily during the "war on terrorism," we who in good conscience cannot go along with these policies, which are not only immoral and insane but also illegal by international law, feel duty-bound to respond to the call of our conscience and stand up in an active way to the stupidity of these atrocious policies.

Some of these people believe that they are called by God to intervene nonviolently in the war preparations that could mean the end of the human race on Earth. In placing themselves between these horrible weapons and their intended use, these individuals are obeying their conscience and challenging the idolatry of a society which seems to worship military power. Often these people believe that the suffering in the world is increased by these policies not only because of killing and the danger of an active war but also because these war policies are robbing our society of resources it could be using to help the hungry, the homeless, the sick, the uneducated, the unemployed in this country and in the world.

Others through a study of our society's problems and the principles of law and justice as means to resolve conflicts nonviolently believe that the development, production, and deployment of genocidal weapons are in fact illegal, that the *United States Constitution* requires the courts to uphold treaties ratified by the U.S. Senate, that preparations for nuclear war are a conspiracy to commit mass murder, genocide, and perhaps even omnicide, the death of everyone. These individuals believe that we as citizens have an obligation in accordance with the Nuremberg Principles not to cooperate with the illegal actions of our government. Thus some have called these direct actions, which are intended to uphold the Nuremberg Principles and challenge the crimes of our government, Nuremberg Actions.

Whatever the reasons people may have for protesting, their support is welcome as long as they are committed to the use of nonviolence as outlined in the Nonviolence Guidelines. Many people believe for a variety of reasons relating to the control of our society by the corporate media and incumbent politicians who are corrupted by the iron triangle of the military-industrial-government complex, that the best thing we can do at this time in history to help save our civilization is to take our power back from our criminal government by acting directly rather than merely symbolically, as in free speech. From this point of view, only such self-sacrifice can hope to awaken the sleeping conscience of our materialistic society.

Thus instead of referring to these actions as civil disobedience, we now understand that we are acting to uphold the laws of God and international law when our government is involved in serious violations of them. (These legal theories will be explained more fully below in the section "International Law and Nuclear Weapons.") Thus we refer to these actions as civil obedience or divine obedience.

Nonviolent protests may take the form of seeming to violate minor laws and being placed under arrest. Affinity groups may walk onto a military base at the main gate or stop traffic in the road from entering a base or perhaps undertake more creative actions to raise people's awareness about these concerns. The reason these actions are not illegal is because they are justified by the circumstances—namely that we have a duty to attempt to stop crimes from being perpetrated and to stop an overwhelming danger which threatens our lives as well as others. A criminal conspiracy (the military) has no right to arrest people simply because they are attempting to point out to people that they are involved in a criminal conspiracy.

In a constitutional form of government, conflicts are supposed to be handled according to due process of the law. That means that when people appear to be violating the law, they are to be taken into custody and brought before a judge to determine if they were in fact guilty of a violation. However, we know from experience that sometimes police may beat people up or handle them roughly in making arrests. Nevertheless in most nonviolent demonstrations where the tone is peaceful, these are the exceptions rather than the common practice.

Those who actively protest and risk arrest must realize that they are going to be thrown into the legal system with all its complexity. During this process individuals are given many choices to make. By understanding different options and their probable consequences, people can make wiser choices.

* *

Whoever advises a leader according to the Way
opposes conquest by force of arms.
The use of force tends to rebound....
Violence is contrary to the Way.
Whatever is contrary to the Way will soon perish.
Weapons are tools of destruction hated by people.
Therefore followers of the Way never use them....
The best soldier is not violent.
The best fighter is not angry....
Those brave in killing will be killed.
Those brave in not killing will live....
For love wins all battles and is the strongest defense.
Heaven gives love to save and protect.
Lao-zi

* *

Arrest

Those who decide to place themselves in a situation where arrest is likely need to prepare themselves carefully for the ordeal. In line with the Nonviolence Guidelines they should make sure that they are carrying no weapons and have no drugs or alcohol on their person. At least one person who is not risking arrest should know their names and pertinent information.

Once one has entered an arrest situation, it can occur at any time. However, there is often a warning given by the law enforcement officer; if so, this is usually the last opportunity to avoid arrest. At the time of arrest, one is usually handcuffed and asked to walk with the officer. Everyone has the choice to cooperate with the arresting officer or not. The extent of noncooperation is up to each individual. Some may go limp so that the officers must carry or drag the person. Those who do not cooperate with the arrest may be given the additional charge of resisting arrest, and they may suffer physical punishment, such as the use of pain holds designed to make a person cooperate. Noncooperation is a tactic that can be used at any time when in custody.

Police are not required to read one the Miranda rights unless they are going to ask questions about the alleged crime. Everyone has the right to remain silent. Remembering the details of the arrest may be helpful in a trial. Everyone has a right to a lawyer and can request one at any time.

Those arrested may be taken to a building or police station for booking. Sometimes people may be released before even being charged. At booking individuals are charged with a specific violation. There are two primary legal systems in this country—the state and the federal government. If the process continues, one will find oneself in one system or the other. In nonviolent protests in which property damage is avoided, the charges are almost always a misdemeanor (state) or a petty offense (federal). The maximum possible sentence is usually either six months and a $500 fine or sometimes one year and a $1000 fine. During booking one is usually asked for information, such as name, address, telephone, social security number, birth date, etc. Those who refuse to give their names may be held longer than others.

Often they ask one to sign a citation promising to appear in court on a specific date, or sometimes they may require bail money before releasing one. Those who sign the citation or pay the bail will be released. Those who refuse to sign or pay the bail may be held in jail or they may be released anyway. If a person remains in custody, arraignment usually occurs fairly soon, within a few days. This is a way of speeding up the whole process and pressuring the system to release people without bail or promises to appear. If people stay in jail, men and women are usually separated.

Solidarity

As Benjamin Franklin once said of the patriots who were declaring their independence from Britain, "We must indeed all hang together, or, most assuredly, we shall all hang separately." This conveys the idea of solidarity. The more people can "hang together" the stronger is their political power in relation to the system. Jails are designed to make people feel powerless and at the mercy of the system. However, when a group works together, they can exert a much greater leverage on that system, especially if it is a jail system already overcrowded and over-burdened or a government already hugely in debt and in need of money to cover its law-enforcement expenses.

Thus in the past many peace activists have refused to pay bail or fines to the system which is oppressing them. This is not only to be in solidarity with each other but also to be in solidarity with all the poor people who cannot afford to buy their way out of jail. In California these tactics have been rather successful in avoiding bail and fines and also long sentences. Of course, the numbers are a major factor in solidarity, but the principles remain the same; and many activists refuse to pay on principle even if they must suffer for it alone. It has been suggested that individuals who feel they cannot spend time in jail might want to consider contributing money to the peace movement and doing support work instead of getting arrested in a symbolic protest and paying money to the government.

In addition to refusing to pay bail or a fine, another common solidarity issue is to refuse to accept probation. This is done so that the movement can grow and not have future actions stifled by the threats of probation revocation. With probation most of the sentence is usually suspended; but if the person is convicted again during the probation, then the suspended jail time can be given from the past action in addition to the new one.

The tactics of refusing to pay a fine or accept probation leave the judge with what he or she often considers less satisfactory choices. All that is really left is community service or time in jail. Community service is becoming more popular, but it still does not give the government back any of the money it spent on law enforcement and courts. Also if community service is refused or not considered serious enough, then the only alternative is jail, which costs the government even more money. Thus the willingness of activists to go to jail can put pressure on the government far beyond the numbers involved could exert in just about any other nonviolent way.

Other solidarity goals may include the objective that past offenders get the same punishment as new offenders, although this can be difficult to achieve. Additional tactics for achieving this or to add pressure to the government to change its policies, can be to plead not guilty and have trials or to engage in various forms of noncooperation while in jail. These may include fasting, not giving information, singing, refusing to walk or get dressed, etc.

Pleading

Arraignment is when one is formally charged in court before a judge by a prosecuting attorney. The judge will ask, "How do you plead to this charge?" The defendant has four possible pleas. Both guilty and no contest are treated as a guilty plea, but by saying that one does not contest the charges one is not actually admitting any guilt. The no contest plea cannot be used as evidence of wrongdoing in a civil suit. The judge usually accepts the no contest plea as though it were a guilty plea. These pleas are then usually followed by sentencing. At this point one has the opportunity to speak as to why one did it, what mitigating circumstances apply, and what sentence might be appropriate. This time for elocution is also an opportunity to express one's feelings or religious beliefs or even make a political speech.

The other two pleas are not guilty and what is called a creative plea, which is simply to say nothing or anything one wishes, which will be treated as a not guilty plea. If it is not a very brief statement, one can expect to be cut off by the judge. The judge is required to enter a not guilty plea unless the defendant clearly pleads either guilty or no contest. As long as one pleads not guilty, they must either proceed with a trial or drop the charges.

After a not guilty plea the judge usually releases the defendants on their own recognizance (OR). However, bail may be required. Those who do not pay bail or sign a bail bond have to stay in jail until the trial.

****

The time has come, or is about to come,
when only large-scale civil disobedience,
which should be nonviolent,
can save the populations from the universal death
which their governments are preparing for them.
Bertrand Russell

Trial

In the federal system one is usually arraigned before a federal magistrate. Magistrates have been appointed, because there are not enough federal judges to handle all of the cases. One has a right to a trial before a federal judge, although one can accept the magistrate as a presiding judge. Because of a Supreme Court ruling, the federal government does not give jury trials on petty offenses where the maximum sentence is six months or less even though the U.S. Constitution states twice that all criminal trials are to be by jury. If one is found guilty by a magistrate and decides to appeal, it is then heard by the federal judge. However, if one has been found guilty by the judge, the first appeal goes to the U.S. Circuit Court of Appeals. Appeal from the Circuit Court would go to the U.S. Supreme Court, though they do not have to hear the case. Other than appeal, the trial before a magistrate or a federal judge will be similar.

In most states the right to trial by a jury is granted. In jury selection the lawyers have the right to question prospective jurors and have individuals dismissed if the judge agrees that they cannot be fair. In addition each side is given a certain number of peremptory challenges which can be used to dismiss individual jurors without giving any reason at all. In a jury trial the judge still makes all rulings on questions of law and instructs the jury as to what the law is. The judge will not allow the jury to hear evidence or testimony that is ruled irrelevant or inadmissible. However, the final verdict and interpretation of the evidence and facts are decided by the jury and must be (in most states) unanimous (consensus), or else it is declared a mistrial because of a hung jury. After a mistrial, defendants may or may not be tried again by a new jury. In other respects a jury trial and a bench or court trial tend to be fairly similar. Since a single judge gives the verdict in a bench trial, there is no chance for a hung jury; it will be either not guilty or guilty.

Everyone has the right to be represented by a lawyer. One can hire a lawyer of one's own choosing. Sometimes several defendants are tried to together and may share the same lawyer. If one is too poor to hire a lawyer, the court will appoint a public defender if one requests it. As long as one is mentally competent, one has the right to represent oneself (pro se or pro per) and be one's own lawyer. This gives one all the privileges of the lawyer in the courtroom, but one is still expected to follow the proper procedures and little allowance may be made for the lack of legal training and knowledge. However, in political trials activists often find that they can represent their concerns better than a lawyer who is unfamiliar with their issues.

There may be a pre-trial hearing for motions some-time between arraignment and the trial date, but if neither side has submitted a motion, it may be canceled. After the jury has been selected in a state trial, the state and federal trial formats are similar.

The prosecuting attorney begins with an opening statement which presents a summary of the case and the evidence in verbal form. Then the lawyer for the defendant may make an opening statement or wait until the prosecution has presented their witnesses. However, in federal court the judge may insist that the defense's opening statement be given immediately after the prosecution's or not at all. The opening statement is supposed to focus on what the evidence will show. If the opening wanders beyond that subject, the judge may interrupt. If the judge believes the evidence being discussed is irrelevant, the attorney may argue a theory of defense to show that it is relevant. This is called an offer of proof. If there is a jury, they will be dismissed as the judge listens to this argument and then rules as to whether that evidence and testimony will be allowed. This is where the defense of necessity and international law may be argued and then probably will be prohibited. Sometimes attorneys never mention this defense in the opening, but it comes up during the questioning of witnesses. At that point if the prosecution or the judge objects, the jury may be removed and the offer of proof presented and ruled on. One is allowed to call expert witnesses to help persuade the judge of the validity of the theory of defense, but they will not be heard by the jury unless the evidence is ruled admissible.

Following the opening statement, the prosecution begins to call their witnesses and question them on the stand. During direct examination of a witness on one's own side, attorneys are not allowed to ask leading questions. Questions must be asked in such a way as not to suggest what the answer ought to be. After the prosecutor has questioned each witness, the defense is allowed to cross-exam them on the issues and evidence that has been presented. During cross-examination of opposing witnesses, attorneys are allowed to ask leading questions, such as "Isn't it true that ..." or "Wouldn't it be fair to say that ..." Cross-examination is an opportunity to expose the errors or confusion or even lack of credibility of witnesses by pointing out contradictions or weaknesses in their testimony. Once the prosecution has presented all their witnesses and physical evidence, then they rest. At this point the defense often presents a motion for dismissal because of lack of evidence. This is routinely denied.

Next the defense calls their witnesses and presents evidence. They have the right to subpoena witnesses and compel them to testify if their testimony is relevant to the case. Defendants have a right to remain silent and are not required to present any defense whatsoever and still may be found not guilty. This is because the burden of proof is on the prosecution to prove that someone committed an illegal act beyond a reasonable doubt or to a moral certainty. Though defendants are not required to testify, activists usually do choose to testify in order to tell their story of what they did and why they did it. Of course, the prosecution then has the right to cross-examine. Sometimes also either side may have additional questions after cross-examination in what is called redirect; again leading questions are still not allowed in redirect. Re-direct may be followed by re-cross. Defendants who are representing themselves pro se usually are allowed to testify in a narrative way, instead of trying to ask themselves questions. This can make it easier to get in some points before objection is heard from the prosecutor or before the judge interrupts. Pro se defendants may gain some advantage, because they can hardly be expected to know all the legal rules; but on the other hand, their lack of knowledge can be a disadvantage in keeping the prosecution honest also.

After the defense has presented their witnesses, the trial proceeds to closing arguments. Because the prosecution has the burden of proving their case beyond a reasonable doubt, they are usually given the first and last speech in the closing. Attorneys are given most leeway in their closing arguments. Rarely is an objection heard from the other side, and the judge is usually reluctant to interrupt a closing argument. One is allowed to wax eloquent and even quote from books. However, one should keep in mind the patience and forbearance of the judge and jury. Opening and closing arguments are opportunities to speak directly to the jury or judge. A pro se defendant thus has great latitude in attempting to move the jury or judge in this speech. To be effective the closing argument needs to rebut the arguments and case presented by the prosecution and do it in such a way that the rebuttal will still stand even after the prosecution presents their last rebuttal.

Having heard the closing arguments, the judge will verbally instruct the jury as to their duty in deliberation and will read and interpret the relevant laws for them. The jury will then retire to a private room to deliberate until they reach a verdict. In a bench trial the judge will give the verdict. If the verdict is not guilty defendants are free to go out and celebrate. If the verdict is guilty, the jury will be dismissed before the sentencing. As with no contest and guilty pleas, defendants who have been found guilty have the right of elocution prior to the passing of sentence. At this time the defendants may indicate their preferences and circumstances in relation to punishment. It is another opportunity to give a speech to the judge.

Defendants who have been sentenced may be taken into custody. If an appeal is going to be filed, one can ask that the sentence be suspended until the appeal is decided.

Jail

Those who go to jail for misdemeanors are usually housed in local facilities. State and federal prisons are generally designed for those who are serving a year or more. The federal government often pays local facilities to keep their prisoners. Activists are often introduced to jails at the time of arrest, and the sentence is just more of the same.

Prisoners are carefully searched, often asked to strip naked and usually given jail clothes. Some facilities spray new inmates for vermin. Since most jails in the United States are very overcrowded, many are under court orders to release people before the full period of their sentence. Days spent in jail at the time of arrest are usually counted. Men and women are separated. Basically the state provides room and board, and inmates have much free time within their restricted areas. One can usually get books, sometimes from the outside also, writing or drawing materials. For many the worst aspect is the noise and especially the television in the day room. Sometimes inmates are asked to work. There is an international tradition that political prisoners are not required to work, but since local authorities may not consider protestors political prisoners, one may face disciplinary confinement for refusing to work. However, often only trustees work, and it is considered a privilege to gain a few small freedoms. Inmates may receive and send mail and also have visitors according to the routine of the jail. Money is placed in a commissary account, and certain items such as snack food, paper, pencils, stamps, envelopes, toilet items, or cigarettes may be purchased.

For many, jail can be a time of deep reflection on one's life and society. One often meets interesting people who for one reason or another do not conform to our society's customs. For some, jail may be a difficult experience. As with anything, one's own attitude is a major factor in determining the value of the experience. Some even believe that given the horrible policies of our government it is the only appropriate place to be.

* *

Nonviolence is the greatest force at the disposal of humanity.
It is mightier than the mightiest weapon of destruction
devised by human ingenuity....
If the mad race for armaments continues,
it is bound to result in a slaughter
such as has never occurred in history.
If there is a victor left, the very victory will be
a living death for the nation that emerges victorious.

There is no escape from the impending doom
save through a bold and unconditional acceptance
of the nonviolent method with all its glorious implications.
Mahatma Gandhi

* *

The survival of democracy depends on the renunciation of violence
and the development of nonviolent means
to combat evil and advance the good....
Only the nonviolent can apply therapy to the violent.
A. J. Muste

* *

Defense of Necessity

In challenging the immoral policies of our government many people are turning to the defense of necessity and international law, because they believe that the U.S. Government is the one who is committing criminal acts. These two defenses which can be used in combination with each other are called affirmative or justification defenses, because instead of merely attempting to deny that one did the minor violation, they are arguing that emergency circumstances justified the seeming violation of a minor law in order to attempt to stop a greater criminal act or to prevent a serious danger from occurring.

As affirmative defenses, the defense must undertake the obligation of proving that a reasonable person would believe each of the five elements that would justify such behavior. For judges to allow any evidence based on these theories of defense, they must be convinced that the defendants have a reasonable chance of proving their case if the evidence were to be allowed. Therefore a verbal offer of proof is usually requested in order to describe the evidence the defendants would present on their behalf if given the chance. Sometimes during the offer of proof, expert witnesses may be called and even asked leading questions in order to establish the case. If the judge rules out this defense, none of this testimony may be heard by the jury.

The necessity defense has been a part of common law in England and has become an established principle in U.S. criminal law. In United States v. Ashton, 24 Fed Case 873 (1834) the crew was found to be justified in refusing to obey a captain's order to continue sailing when they acted upon a "bona fide reasonable belief" that the ship was unseaworthy. The Ashton case established that "not just peril, but a well-founded belief in impending peril is sufficient to raise the defense."

There are five elements in the defense of necessity, each of which must be proven:

1. There is a danger or harm.
2. The danger is imminent.
3. Other methods have been inadequate to remove the danger.
4. The action taken was a lesser evil than the danger.
5. A reasonable person would believe that this action could remove the danger.

International Law Defense

The international law defense may be combined with the defense of necessity by substituting violations of international law for the danger in each of the five elements. Thus defendants felt obligated to act in order to prevent the commission of crimes.

The judicial system of the United States is required to apply international law and U.S. treaties as is stated in the U.S. Constitution Article III Section 2: "The judicial power shall extend to all cases, in law and equity, arising under this Constitution, the laws of the United States, and treaties made, or which shall be made, under their authority." Article VI makes it even clearer that international law as defined by treaties that the U.S. has entered into are to be the highest law along with the Constitution and are to take precedent over any other laws:

This Constitution and the laws of the United States
which shall be made in pursuance thereof and all treaties made,
or which shall be made, under the authority of the United States,
shall be the supreme law of the land;
and the judges in every State shall be bound thereby,
anything in the Constitution or laws of any state
to the contrary notwithstanding.

The U.S. Supreme Court in Paquete Habana, 175 US 677, (1900) stated,

International law is part of our law,
and must be ascertained and administered
by the courts of justice of appropriate jurisdiction
as often as questions of right depending upon it
are duly presented for their determination.

The following are some of the U.S. treaties and generally accepted principles of international law that can be used in presenting this defense:

* Treaty of Renunciation of War as a National Policy, sometimes referred to as the Kellogg-Briand Pact or the Pact of Paris, signed August 27, 1928 by fifteen powers including the U.S. The treaty was ratified by the U.S. Senate on December 4, 1928 with only one dissenting vote. Compatible with the United Nations, it is still in force in 62 nations as of 1969:

Deeply sensible of their solemn duty
to promote the welfare of mankind;
persuaded that the time has come
when a frank renunciation of war
as an instrument of national policy should be made
to the end that the peaceful and friendly relations
now existing between their peoples may be perpetuated;
convinced that all changes in their relations with one another
should be sought only by pacific means
and be the result of a peaceful and orderly process,
and that any signatory power which shall hereafter seek
to promote its national interests by resort to war
should be denied the benefits furnished by this treaty;
hopeful that, encouraged by their example,
all the other nations of the world will join in this humane endeavor
and by adhering to the present treaty as soon as it comes into force
bring their peoples within the scope of its beneficent provisions,
thus uniting the civilized nations of the world
in a common renunciation of war
as an instrument of their national policy;
have decided to conclude a treaty ...
Article 1. The high contracting parties solemnly declare
in the names of their respective peoples
that they condemn recourse to war
for the solution of international controversies,
and renounce it as an instrument of national policy
in their relations with one another.
Article 2. The high contracting parties agree
that the settlement or solution of all disputes
or conflicts of whatever nature or of whatever origin they may be,
which may arise among them,
shall never be sought except by pacific means....

* The United Nations Charter was signed June 26, 1945 and by votes of both houses of the U.S. Congress the United States became an official member on December 20, 1945:

We the peoples of the United Nations
determined to save succeeding generations
from the scourge of war,
which twice in our lifetime has brought untold sorrow to mankind,
and to reaffirm faith in fundamental human rights,
in the dignity and worth of the human person,
in the equal rights of men and women
and of nations large and small,
and to establish conditions under which justice
and respect for the obligations arising from treaties
and other sources of international law can be maintained,
and to promote social progress
and better standards of life in larger freedom,
and for these ends to practice tolerance
and live together in peace with one another as good neighbors,
and to unite our strength to maintain
international peace and security,
and to ensure, by the acceptance of principles
and the institution of methods, that armed force shall not be used,
save in the common interest,
and to employ international machinery for the promotion
of the economic and social advancement of all peoples,
have resolved to combine our efforts to accomplish these aims ...
Article 1. The Purposes of the United Nations are:
  1. To maintain international peace and security,
and to that end: to take effective collective measures
for the prevention and removal of threats to the peace,
and for the suppression of acts of aggression
or other breaches of the peace,
and to bring about by peaceful means,
and in conformity with the principles

of justice and international law,
adjustment or settlement of international disputes
or situations which might lead to a breach of the peace;

2. To develop friendly relations among nations
based on respect for the principle of equal rights
and self-determination of peoples,
and to take other appropriate measures
to strengthen universal peace;

3. To achieve international cooperation
in solving international problems
of an economic, social, cultural, or humanitarian character,
and in promoting and encouraging respect for human rights
and for fundamental freedoms for all
without distinction as to race, sex, language, or religion; and

4. To be a center for harmonizing the actions of nations
in the attainment of these common ends.

Article 2. The Organization and its Members,
in pursuit of the Purposes stated in Article 1,
shall act in accordance with the following Principles:

1. The Organization is based on the principle
of the sovereign equality of its Members.

2. All Members, in order to ensure to all of them
the rights and benefits resulting from membership,
shall fulfill in good faith the obligations assumed by them
in accordance with the present Charter.

3. All Members shall settle their international disputes
by peaceful means in such a manner
that international peace and security,
and justice, are not endangered.

4. All Members shall refrain in their international relations
from the threat or use of force against the territorial integrity
or political independence of any state,
or in any other manner inconsistent
with the Purposes of the United Nations.

* Treaty of London authorizing the Nuremberg War Crimes Tribunals on August 8, 1945 was signed by the U.S. Article 6a states that "waging of a war of aggression" is a "crime against peace" imposing "individual responsibility."

Article 8. The fact that the Defendant acted pursuant to order of his Government or of a superior
shall not free him from responsibility,
but may be considered in mitigation of punishment
if the Tribunal determines that justice so requires.

* Charter of the two War Crimes Tribunals known as the Nuremberg Principles were expressly reaffirmed by unanimous resolution of the United Nations General Assembly in 1946 and, according to international law expert J. L. Brierly, are now undoubtedly accepted as part of general international law:

Principle I. Any person who commits an act
which constitutes a crime under international law
is responsible therefor and liable to punishment.
Principle II. The fact that internal law does not impose a penalty
for an act which constitutes a crime under international law
does not relieve the person who committed the act
from responsibility under international law.
Principle III. The fact that a person committed an act
which constitutes a crime under international law
acted as Head of State or responsible Government official
does not relieve him from responsibility under international law.
Principle IV. The fact that a person acted
pursuant to order of his Government or of a superior
does not relieve him from responsibility under international law,
provided a moral choice was in fact possible to him.
Principle V. Any person charged with a crime
under international law has the right to a fair trial

on the facts and law.

Principle VI. The crimes hereinafter set out are punishable as crimes under international law:

  a. Crimes against peace:

    i. Planning, preparation, initiation or waging of
    a war of aggression or a war in violation
    of international treaties, agreements or assurances;

    ii. Participation in a common plan or conspiracy
    for the accomplishment of any of the acts
    mentioned under (i).

  b. War crimes:

Violations of the laws or customs of war which include,
but are not limited to, murder,
ill-treatment or deportation to slave-labor
or for any other purpose of civilian population
of or in occupied territory,
murder or ill-treatment of prisoners of war
or persons on the seas, killing of hostages,
plunder of public or private property,
wanton destruction of cities, towns, or villages,
or devastation not justified by military necessity.

  c. Crimes against humanity:

Murder, extermination, enslavement, deportation
and other inhuman acts done against any civilian population,
or persecutions on political, racial or religious grounds,
when such acts are done or such persecutions are carried on
in execution of or in connection with any crime against peace
or any war crime.

Principle VII. Complicity in the commission of
a crime against peace, a war crime, or a crime against humanity
as set forth in Principle VI is a crime under international law.

* Geneva Convention Relative to the Protection of Civilian Persons
in Time of War, August 12, 1949, ratified by the U.S. and went
into force February 2, 1956:

Article 27. Protected persons are entitled, in all circumstances,
to respect for their persons, their honor, their family rights,
their religious convictions and practices,
and their manners and customs.
They shall at all times be humanely treated, and shall be protected
specifically against all acts of violence or threats thereof
and against insults and public curiosity.
Women shall be especially protected against any attack
on their honor, in particular against rape, enforced prostitution,
or any form of indecent assault.
Without prejudice to the provisions relating to their state
of health, age and sex, all protected persons shall be treated
with the same consideration by the Party to the conflict
in whose power they are, without any adverse distinction
based, in particular, on race, religion or political opinion.

Article 30. The High Contracting Parties specifically agree
that each of them is prohibited from taking any measure
of such character as to cause physical suffering
or extermination of protected persons in their lands.
This prohibition applies not only to murder, torture,
corporal punishment, mutilation
and medical or scientific experiments not necessitated
by the medical treatment of a protected person,
but also to any other measures of brutality
whether applied by civilian or military agents.

Article 31. No protected person may be punished for an offense
he or she has not personally committed.
Collective penalties and likewise all measures of intimidation
or of terrorism are prohibited.
Pillage is prohibited.
Reprisals against protected persons and their property
are prohibited.

Article 32. The taking of hostages is prohibited.

* Treaty on the Non-Proliferation of Nuclear Weapons done at Washington, London, and Moscow July 1, 1968, ratified by the U.S. Senate and entered into force on March 5, 1970:

The States concluding this Treaty ...
considering the devastation that would be visited upon all mankind
by a nuclear war and the consequent need to make every effort
to avert the danger of such a war
and to take measures to safeguard the security of peoples,
believing that the proliferation of nuclear weapons
would seriously enhance the danger of nuclear war,
in conformity with resolutions of the United Nations
General Assembly calling for the conclusion of an agreement
on the prevention of wider dissemination of nuclear weapons,...
declaring their intention to achieve at the earliest possible date
the cessation of the nuclear arms race
and to undertake effective measures
in the direction of nuclear disarmament,
urging the cooperation of all States
in the attainment of this objective,
recalling the determination expressed by the Parties
to the 1963 Treaty banning nuclear weapon tests
in the atmosphere in outer space and under water
in its Preamble to seek to achieve the discontinuance
of all test explosions of nuclear weapons for all time
and to continue negotiations to this end,
desiring to further the easing of international tension
and the strengthening of trust between States
in order to facilitate the cessation
of the manufacture of nuclear weapons,
the liquidation of all their existing stockpiles,
and the elimination from national arsenals
of weapons and the means of their delivery
pursuant to a treaty on general and complete disarmament
under strict and effective international control,

recalling that,
in accordance with the Charter of the United Nations,
States must refrain in their international relations
from the threat or use of force against the territorial integrity
or political independence of any State,
or in any other manner inconsistent with
the Purposes of the United Nations,
and that the establishment and maintenance
of international peace and security are to be promoted
with the least diversion for armaments
of the world's human and economic resources,
have agreed as follows: ...
Article VI. Each of the Parties to the Treaty undertakes
to pursue negotiations in good faith on effective measures
relating to cessation of the nuclear arms race at an early date
and to nuclear disarmament,
and on a treaty on general and complete disarmament
under strict and effective international control.

War Tax Resistance

Since about half of federal income tax still goes to pay for past, present and future expenses of the military, many activists feel that in good conscience they cannot contribute any money to this effort. The simplest way to do this is to earn less than the minimum amount required in order to owe no federal income tax.

Others, whose incomes are larger, may choose to refuse to pay a portion or all of their income tax owed. This means that the Internal Revenue Service may attempt to take the money from bank accounts, salary checks, or any other way they think they can get it. Individuals are not usually put in jail for refusing to pay, but they occasionally can be found guilty of violating tax laws or perjury laws if subterfuge is used.

The following organizations are able to provide more information:

National War Tax Resistance Coordinating Committee
P. O. Box 6512
Ithaca, NY 14851
607 277-0593
800 269-7464
nwtrcc@lightlink.com
www.nwtrcc.org

War Resisters League
339 Lafayette St.
New York, NY 10012
212 228-0450
wrl@warresisters.org
www.warresisters.org

* *
You shall not kill....
You shall love your neighbor as yourself.
Moses
* *

Blessed are the peacemakers,
for they shall be called the children of God....
You heard that it was said to the ancients, 'You shall not kill,
and whoever kills will be subject to judgment.'
But I tell you that all who are angry at their brother or sister
will be subject to judgment....
You heard that it was said,
'An eye for an eye and a tooth for a tooth.'
But I tell you not to oppose the bad,
but whoever strikes you on the right cheek,
turn to them also the other....
You heard that it was said,
'You shall love your neighbor and hate your enemy.'

But I tell you, 'Love your enemies, do good to those hating you, bless those cursing you, pray about those abusing you.'
Jesus

* *

Building Community

There are many ways that each of us can contribute our skills and assets to the work for peace and justice in this world. In this process it is important that we remain true to ourselves and our own personal relationships. By cooperating together and supporting each other in the many ways people can work on these issues, we can strengthen and improve the quality of our lives and efforts.

By appreciating the work of various people and organizations, we can see how we are part of a larger movement for social change in this country and the world. Establishing peace and justice in the world are such overwhelming challenges that we need to form coalitions with like-minded people, while we each do our little part to make the struggles of so many eventually successful. Ultimately our children and grandchildren will inherit the world we leave them. Let us hope that by our actions, both personal and collective, we will have passed on a planet that is closer to our goals and aspirations. The problems we face, not only in regard to the dangers of war but also with environmental deterioration, call us to special efforts, because it is likely that the next few years will be critical to the future of human civilization and planet Earth. Let us then do our best to be true to ourselves, our communities, our species, our planet, and our God.

World Peace Communications also publishes:

WISDOM BIBLE
Way Power Book (Dao De Jing) by Lao-zi
Two Confucian Classics
Seven *Upanishads*
The Lord's Song (Bhagavad-Gita)
Union Threads (Yoga Sutras) by Patanjali
Buddha's First Sermon
Path of Truth (Dhammapada)
Plato's *Alcibiades, Defense of Socrates, Crito, Phaedo*
Epicurus
Wisdom of Solomon
The Good Message of Jesus the Christ
Manual of Epictetus
The Consolation of Philosophy by Boethius
Qur'an **Selections**
920 pages (hardback $45, paperback $25)

HISTORY OF ETHICS:
Volume 1 To 30 BC: Ancient Wisdom and Folly
877 pages ($30)

Volume 2   30 BC to 1300: Age of Belief
1116 pages ($45)

GUIDES TO PEACE AND JUSTICE
Great Peacemakers
Philosophers of Peace
and World Peace Advocates
993 pages ($25)

Complete texts of all these books and other writings by Sanderson Beck are available on his website at **san.beck.org**.